Of Media and People

Of Media and People

Everette E. Dennis

SAGE Publications
International Educational and Professional Publisher
Newbury Park   London   New Delhi

For information address:

SAGE Publications, Inc.
2455 Teller Road
Newbury Park, California 91320

SAGE Publications Ltd.
6 Bonhill Street
London EC2A 4PU
United Kingdom

SAGE Publications India Pvt. Ltd.
M-32 Market
Greater Kailash I
New Delhi 110 048 India

Printed in the United States of America

Library of Congress Cataloguing-in-Publication Data

Dennis, Everette E.
    Of media and people / Everette E. Dennis.
        p.   cm.
    Includes bibliographical references and index.
    ISBN 0-8039-4746-1.—ISBN 0-8039-4747-X (pbk.)
    1. Mass media.   2. Journalism.   I. Title.
P91.D447   1992
302.23—dc20   92-28903

92 93 94 95 96   10 9 8 7 6 5 4 3 2 1

Sage Production Editor: Astrid Virding

Contents

Acknowledgments

As with other research and writing I've done in a number of authored and edited books, I am grateful for the help of several vital individuals. With this book I am especially indebted to Dirk A. Smillie, who helped assemble the material and who did considerable editing. Donna Lee Van Cott also deserves recognition for her assistance with a variety of tasks connected with this book. Several specific essays were possible only because of research assistants Jon Vanden Heuvel, Alfred Evans, and Seth Rachlin. Earlier, David Stebenne was also involved in projects related to the essays and commentaries.

I am also grateful to The Freedom Forum Media Studies Center at Columbia University and to my colleagues at our parent foundation, The Freedom Forum. Our many conversations and spirited discussions have improved this work.

—EVERETTE E. DENNIS

Introduction

Nothing is more crucial to the mass media than their relationship with their audiences. Though particular media sometimes seem to emerge and evolve with little immediate consideration for their readers, viewers, or users, that condition does not long remain if the given medium is to survive.

It is not uncommon for the creative individuals who give us new newspapers, magazines, or television programs to say that they are producing the work for themselves and people like them. That, however, is rarely the case because, increasingly, new media do not appear without a great deal of planning or forethought, typically supported by market research. Planning plays a vital role these days as those who supply the capital to create new media have exacting standards for their investments.

The fragile relationship between media and people is played out in a crowded marketplace in which new ventures exist alongside venerable media and a limited number can and will survive. Just what standard determines the success or failure of what are now called "new media products" may depend on many things. Typically, a simple profit and loss statement at the end of a circumscribed period will tell the story, but not always. Some new media ventures are calibrated to accept losses for several years before they actually get into the black. A few others may never make a profit, but will be satisfying enough to their owners—either individuals or corporations with deep pockets—that they may live for years fueled more by ego than by the bottom line. A few years ago, for example, a new magazine for middle-aged persons with the unfortunate name of *Second Wind* appeared on magazine racks. The owners' high hopes notwithstanding, the magazine did not attract sufficient capital to continue beyond a pilot issue. Obviously it had no "second wind."

Most, if not all, of the conflicts, controversies, and incidents that become the stuff of media criticism and reporting are related to the people-media connection. Sometimes the connections between media and their audiences are fragile, such as television ratings, which can

1

kill a superb new show within weeks. Others have a less demanding threshold and can hang on for years before disappointing demographics or viewership pull the plug. Naturally, the media-people connection is not a simple linear relationship, but is filtered through the institution of advertising or is shaped by distribution systems or the legal-regulatory system. This book represents an effort to sort out, closely examine, and assess several critical arenas of media-people relationships that have consequences for the public. The material presented here is drawn from nearly fifty articles, columns, speeches, and commentaries developed by me in my role as executive director of the Gannett Foundation Media Center at Columbia University, which got a new moniker—The Freedom Forum Media Studies Center—in 1991, when our parent foundation divested itself of 15 million shares of Gannett Co., Inc. stock and surrendered the name Gannett in the process. As the head of a media studies center—a think tank that scopes out matters related to mass communication and technological change—I get frequent opportunities to be a sound bite on national television and to write and speak on media matters. In the process of doing this, I draw on two essential kinds of knowledge: that derived from the works of scholars and that which emerges from experience in the field by professionals and leaders of industry. I do this through continuous contacts with scholars and media professionals as well as other citizens in the United States and abroad who care deeply about the communication system we live with and who typically want it to get better.

This book has seven parts, each assembling material from the sources mentioned above, most of it heavily edited, rewritten and combined with various strands and ideas in a career that has given me a rare catbird seat in both the industry and academic arenas. At the same time, my colleagues and I are privileged to see and feel media-people relationships through the prism of institutional life, wherein links between media and such fields as education, business, labor, the military, and others are very much under scrutiny.

These essays begin with a section on media performance—the bottom line for many so-called media consumers or audience members who know media as they see its content. Many of them are no more interested in the "manufacturing process" that creates it than are consumers of sausage interested in how pork is produced. Clearly, as we point out later, they probably ought to be, but that is not often the case, even though their "information health" may depend on it. The nature of news and information is examined, as are various ethical dilemmas that challenge the quality of what it is we are getting in our media. Although this early section of the book takes most of its cues from our domestic media and the ethnocentric code that governs them, we move quickly to the arena of international or global communication. Here the media machines, the networks, media companies, and individual outlets, are taking on an increasingly global coloration, even though there is still little media content that serves more than one people and one culture. Perhaps the Cable News Network or the British Broadcasting Corporation are exceptions, but even they are mostly the products of nationals of one country with high expectations for international appeal and marketing.

The people on the production line in media organizations—the journalists, editors, producers, and others—are the subject of a section of this book on educating communicators. This is a topic typically in the purview of insiders only, but I try here to indicate why it ought also to be a public concern. Like it or not, our media people play a quasi-public servant role, even though they are, of course, unelected.

People who work in the media and people for whom media are intended need to know and understand a subtle, but important trend in communications—that of convergence of all media into a single electronically based, computer-driven system. As text and data come together with visual images, all media now have more in common than ever before, and the public needs to know more about this new force that is blending and blurring old and new media with extraordinary results.

Earlier commentary about the system that produces news and information is later seen in terms of reporting and reportorial imperatives: that is, what is being covered and why. Here again, general concerns are connected with specifics like election coverage, news of race relations as well as art and culture.

These singular concerns and functions must live in a larger industrial context and that is the subject or our next set of essays, wherein economic issues are applied to such individual communication industries as newspapers and television as well as new media.

A final section of the book looks at what is always the greatest story for any generation, that of war news. As this book was being prepared, the short-lived Persian Gulf War occurred and we made an effort to track it as a media event and as a preoccupation for media and people, thus integrating many of the themes introduced earlier.

This volume was assembled largely at the request of people corresponding with me who asked for copies of various speeches and articles I have written in several venues. Frequently I was urged to "put them together" and connect singular instances with a larger whole. I have done so, selecting from among many more items than one could include here.

In each case I have revisited work done since the late 1980s, and have applied tests of pertinence that ask whether the text has utility for people—interested citizens as well as professionals, scholars, and students. Material that did not, hit the cutting room floor. Readers will note that for historical accuracy names like the Soviet Union have been retained in material written prior to November 1991. Similarly, The Freedom Forum Media Studies Center is called by its former moniker, the Gannett Center for Media Studies, in some instances.

What is presented here builds on an earlier book of essays, *Reshaping the Media*, published in 1990. It is my hope that the essays and commentaries included here will stimulate thought and contribute to what ought to be a continuing conversation between the public, the media, and media people.

—EVERETTE E. DENNIS

PART I

On Media Performance

1. Salvos Without Solutions[†]

Most critics of the media, whether they come from industry or the academy, typically seek improvement in the present model and practice rather than accept or celebrate the status quo. Of course, even the most cheerful of us, when asked to assess and evaluate anything as volatile and controversial as the media industries or journalistic performance, will find something we would like to change. Some among us will want radical reforms while others will be content to embroider around the edges, suggesting only the most modest improvements in a system we believe essentially sound, if not exemplary.

Anyone who pays attention to the history of print and electronic media in the United States knows that our system of communication was not achieved without considerable struggle. At every step in its development, each of the media and their principal characteristics—newspapers and their commitment to impartial reporting, magazines that offer interpretation and analysis, television that traffics in powerful pictures—evolved because hard choices were made against the backdrop of a market economy. Whether we are talking about a Constitution that gives special protection to freedom of expression, an economy that pushes media enterprises toward concentration and corporatization, or the professional standards by which journalists and other media people live, it is clear that our system—for better or worse—has been based on the realities of daily survival in a world where successful media must be profitable, winning favor among consumers immediately and over time.

In the wake of the profound political and economic changes of 1989 to 1990 in Eastern Europe, those who promote freedom (however it is defined in a given country or society) have been looking toward American media and the West for models of success. There is much admiration of our media enterprises, with their large and loyal audiences as well as record returns on profits. As the new

† Lecture given March 22, 1990; The Reed Sarratt Distinguished Lecture, School of Journalism, University of North Carolina, Chapel Hill.

media leadership of Eastern Europe reaches out to the West for aid, it seems to embrace many aspects of our own successful, if imperfect, media system. At the same time Western media leaders are offering aid—some economic, some technical and professional—in an effort to nurture the young and fragile media that are emerging in countries like Poland, Hungary, and Czechoslovakia.

I have spoken to legal scholars who are ready to help rewrite constitutions, economists and entrepreneurs who want to help shape a new media economy, editors and publishers who want to contribute professional expertise as well as technical aid and equipment. Journalism educators have also joined this dialogue, which attempts to connect the yearning of Eastern Europeans for a new regime of freedom of expression with our desire to be genuinely helpful. To be sure, there are those on the left and the right who see this activity as the next stage in an ideological battle, with some gloating over the failure of communism and others eager to rebuild a new worker state. Although the intricacies of this debate are many, the general outline is quite simple. The media systems of Eastern Europe and, increasingly, those of the former Soviet Union, are in turmoil, and many people on both sides of what used to be called the Iron Curtain are eager to do something about it—to play a role in the process of change.

Standing back from this lively and engaging interaction, there is a general conclusion that the U.S. media system, despite its imperfections, looks favorable when compared with most of the rest of the world.

Yet even as this scramble goes on to connect our system (and perhaps even our values) with emerging media enterprises in other countries— a process that reifies and even celebrates our system—there is at the same time a persistent stream of criticism in the United States that questions the direction, structure and viability of our system of communication. Whether this is simply part of the American penchant for constant improvement and change or a genuine dissatisfaction with the present state of things is difficult to determine.

As a student of communication I have long appreciated the yield of media criticism. It has engaged some of our most thoughtful citizens as they have commented on the constitutional authority, economic base, content, performance, ethics and credibility of our media in all their incarnations as they deliver information, opinion, entertainment and advertising.

Even before Horace Greeley's writings of the mid-nineteenth century, there have been great questions posed about media ownership. In a simpler world, Greeley, a one-time utopian who lived at Brook Farm (an 1840s communitarian experiment) but who was in every sense an entrepreneur, talked about employee ownership of his and other newspapers. Later, such editorial giants as William Rockhill Nelson and Lucius Nieman also championed the idea of newspaper employees as owners or shareholders, giving professional newspeople a vested interest in the papers that employed them. As the forces of a market economy later brought us newspaper chains or groups—an arrangement that presaged modern communication empires, some of them global—such owner-editors as William Allen White, Oswald Garrison Villard and others joined this debate, usually warning against bigness and business values.

Over the years the substance of this debate has changed little: "Bigness is bad, concentration is bad, diversity is good," warn the critics. Underlying this critique is the fear that freedom of expression could be choked off by greed. There is speculation that fewer and fewer owners will control more and more of the communication enterprise, thus leading to an arrogant and unresponsive press. Worse yet has been the specter of nonmedia owners, ranging from domestic soap manufacturers and oil companies to foreign investors, especially the Japanese, who hardly hold our values dear and who might "contaminate" the media, thus impairing freedom. This venerable criticism is also quite contemporary. Although we often associate these sentiments with critics like Ben Bagdikian, Noam Chomsky or Herbert Schiller—and a host of more obscure voices—some of these same ideas are also echoed in the media community itself.

In the early 1970s I heard a speech by John Cowles Jr., who warned that too much media power in the hands of a single owner might be dangerous. He did not like the growth of big media companies, although he himself headed a small chain of newspapers, broadcasting stations, and other enterprises, including, at the time, a market research firm, a magazine and a book publisher. Cowles thought that a single owner should only control properties in communities where it (or its agents) could have a real presence. He stopped short of urging more rigorous enforcement of antitrust laws (or the introduction of new and stiffer ones). This speech ignited a debate, with some commentators saying large media companies could establish a significant "presence" in any community where they owned media and might even offer a more professional "product" than many family owned firms had in the past. Others praised Cowles for what they musingly called his "death of capitalism" speech. And there were some who thought his ideas self-serving, since his notions would leave his own company untouched while others would have to divest extensive holdings. Still, he dared to say what others in the newspaper business did not.

Cowles' speech was thoughtful, brave, and most of all, unusual. Not only did it offer an assessment of ownership issues and problems but it also proposed a modest solution. That, I would later learn, was rare indeed in the annals of media criticism, which fires many salvos but offers few solutions.

More recently, some of the most thoughtful leaders of the communication industry have continued to comment on the present state and probable future of the media industries. James Ottaway Jr., scion of Ottaway Newspapers, a small group now owned by Dow Jones, where he is a senior officer, often worried aloud about media concentration and freedom of expression. He decried some corporate practices and urged more attention to long-term thinking and editorial nourishment for news organizations. The late C. K. McClatchy, owner of a respected chain of newspapers in the West, similarly raised questions about the quality of the news media and criticized media groups whose enterprises he felt needed improvement.

More recently, Rance Crain of the business magazines by the same name, including *Advertising Age,* gave a riveting speech in which he decried in detail the negative effects of Wall Street practices on the communication industry.

About the same time that Ottaway, McClatchy and others seemed to be joining the longstanding scholar-critic debate on the structure and ownership of U.S. media, changes in ownership at all three of America's great broadcast networks sparked a torrent of criticism, most often coming from news division employees who decried corporate practices that value short-term profits over long-term investments. Such practices, they argued, diminished editorial quality and debased broadcasting. During a period of substantial downsizing, not only at the networks but also at newsmagazines, I spoke with many disgruntled, displaced employees about what they called the decline of news and the end of a golden era of national broadcasting. Later I would hear from many like-minded persons from magazines and book publishing who also spoke bitterly about the changing (and they would say disintegrating) nature of their industries. They, too, argued that editorial intuition and public interest news were being replaced by market-oriented offerings, more often than not the handiwork of MBAs with little interest in or appreciation for news.

Several books about CBS alone spell out a scenario of gloom and doom in which they claim the public is the big loser in this high-stakes game.

The ownership changes that put Larry Tisch in charge at CBS, the team of Tom Murphy and Daniel Burke at Capital Cities/ABC, and General Electric's Robert Wright at NBC, were quickly eclipsed by an announcement in 1989 that the giant firms of Time Inc. and Warner Communications were about to merge. In a corporate drama involving Paramount Communications and the Delaware Chancery Court, the merger was consummated, raising to a significant level of discussion the dual trends of globalism and giantism that seemed to be sweeping the media. In the 1980s, giant media firms emerged in Germany, France, Italy, Japan, and the United States. Wall Street analysts said this was a natural development in an increasingly global economy. Always someone asked, "What will be the consequences of this growth and development?" Consequences for whom, of course, is an essential clarification. But beyond that glib response, no one really knew what would work economically, not to mention the potential impact, if any, on existing media industries or new ones that might spring up.

Responses to the Time-Warner merger and subsequent indications of global-giant developments have been mixed. Some cheer them on as "pump primers" in what is increasingly an international service economy, while others conjure some of the perennial arguments mentioned earlier.

Joining the clash of critics and market analysts are a few media scholars who variously look for links between ownership and editorial content, between professionalism and control, between corporate values and what they term *traditional editorial* values. They have produced a still thin but growing literature, though, to date, its yield has few clear answers. Often, studies are based on a single-newspaper or a single-media group, usually out of context and without connections to trends in other industries. Empirical studies over nearly forty years have produced no smoking gun to prove conclusively that content was debased by ownership. There was, however, some modest evidence that group ownership produces less diversity in editorial endorsements.

More recently, critical scholars who question capitalism as a basis for the media system have also emerged. This little-recognized movement is the journalism school equivalent of critical legal studies, a force in legal education that has caused a deep rift at many leading law schools. Thus this new qualitative dimension joins more systematic, empirical studies as well as a long history of legal-historical analysis and other more polemical discussions of what is wrong with U.S. media. Inasmuch as there are courses on this topic—some of which I have taught—and books that inventory the literature of media criticism—at least one of which I have written—I will not dwell here on the complex contours of this intriguing field of inquiry. I will say, though, that when one asks for the bottom line, the critics are much better at telling us what is wrong than they are at telling us what should be done about it.

There are those who would impose government as an arbiter; others who would change our governmental and economic system. But in the main there is mostly a lament with few workable proposals for change that would, on behalf of the public, improve the media system, its internal structure or its yield. Predictably, people with little power have one view while those who are in command have only the most cursory suggestions to change a system they fret about, in spite of its success.

Though I have dwelled on those from industry and from the academy who assess our media system and find it lacking, there are also many enthusiastic industry leaders who give company pep talks pointing up the glories of our system and its contributions to freedom of expression. And it might be added that the field of journalism education has far more professors who identify with the industry and its values than it has detractors who are disappointed with it. Well beyond these commentators, who are as predictable as the purveyors of gloom and doom, are other analysts and critics who see profoundly positive indicators in the general growth of media and media companies. With the decline of the networks has come an array of new offerings from cable and broadcast groups. With the decline of newsmagazines have come other national media that strengthen rather than weaken news sources available to the public. Critics also hail the technological revolution that has enhanced traditional media as well as stimulated the growth of "new media," some of them the result of desktop publishing and other innovations. Surely, they argue, this advances diversity. Amid these trends it should be noted that even disaffected observers of American media are reluctant to say that editorial content overall is on the downslide. From judges of the Pulitzer Prizes to average readers and viewers, there seems to be a consensus that the press and news media, like the movies, are getting "better than ever." The warnings about the diminution of diversity of content seem to be just that— warnings about what might happen, not a statement about the present—although concentration of ownership is a reality. Still, even concentration does not put media companies in a few hands but in the collective hands of many shareholders, including pension funds, universities and other private and societal interests. Professionalism seems on the rise, not on the wane, and the great media companies increasingly talk of methods that will yield greater "customer service and satisfaction" rather than less.

I will not belabor the upbeat analysis that counters a gloomy and depressing view, but I would like to return to the long and, I think, honorable and well-intentioned assessment of our media that often finds their flaws and foibles. At one level much of this criticism is useful. It alerts us to potential problems that could jeopardize democratic communication. It is such criticism that brings the Congress into constructive dialogue with communication industry leaders.

Much of this criticism purports to stand for "the public interest" as opposed to private gain and has sparked important debates about quality in our news, opinion, and entertainment media. When a caring critic decries a practice that diminishes the credibility of television news or points out a newspaper's poor coverage of an event, it might just be useful for the media to respond and let the public in on the conversation. I once heard an editor tell his staff that when they took a call from a complaining reader, they ought to respond as though the conversation were being played on the radio. Maybe some of these daily discussions ought to be played where the public can tune in and appreciate the process of feedback. I can think of scores of less-than-admirable media practices in an imperfect world that were modified because of a useful conversation between consumers and newspeople.

But, at the same time, I wonder about the pertinence of sweeping societal criticism of the media that would dismantle some media corporations, alter the relationship between media and government, or challenge the viability of national media versus those destined to be more global. Few critics link their dire diagnoses with clear-headed proposals for change or other solutions to problems, new and longstanding. When some of the most negative of them are asked, "Well, what should we do about this?" they do not rush to Congress asking for a new regime of regulation. They do not push the Justice Department for more rigorous enforcement of antitrust laws. And they certainly do not urge the IRS to be more attentive.

In short, many critics are not particularly interested in intervening in a system they are quite happy to deplore. Some of them even argue that their role is like that of the movie critic, to assess what is offered by theaters, not to produce new and better films. Perhaps so, although I am inclined to think that those who find so much fault do have some responsibility to suggest alternatives. And I think that critics in the academy, especially, in the name of intellectual honesty and scholarly context, owe their readers competent comparisons with media systems elsewhere in the world. A few critics do suggest tax incentives for family owned enterprises and rewards for those who do significant minority hiring or foster minority ownership, but for the most part there is a paucity of prescription in a world in which every person can be a critic.

Only recently has there been an important vote of confidence in our media system, flaws and all, by analysts and critics who are being called on to advise the new and emerging media of Eastern Europe. Where do they get their examples? From our own system. Certainly some critics on the left would prefer to see a media system develop without flaws but nevertheless they, too, have joined in a trendy media crusade to assist and comfort people in a region that was all but cut off from international communication for nearly forty years. No doubt, as with the reindustrialization of Germany and Japan after World War II, there are opportunities to build new communication systems that are philosophically linked to national and cultural roots, organized around appropriate and creative in-frastructures, blessed with modern technology and new equipment, and operated by a new generation of professionals who, while benefiting from our aid and example, will invent new ways of communicating with their peoples and the rest of the world.

Those in Eastern Europe, the Soviet Union, China, and even Central America who will necessarily fashion new media and new media structures can also benefit us if we join in constructive dialogue with

them. Our own system and way of doing business evolved over two
centuries of incremental change, sometimes spurred by such forces
as the industrial revolution or the information age, but rarely required to grapple at one time with the kinds of profound changes
that swept the world in 1989-1990. What an extraordinary time we
live in when it is possible to ask simultaneously:

- What kind of media law and governmental regime best foster freedom
  of expression?
- What kinds of economic arrangements are most beneficial to an active
  and vibrant media system?
- How should executives and managers run media enterprises?
- What should be the professional standard by which an ideal media
  system and organization live?
- What kinds of feedback mechanisms will assure that a media system
  truly serves its society, country and community?
- What mode of training and professional education assures a high-caliber
  work force?
- To what extent are research and development necessary to the longev-
  ity and responsiveness of a new media industry?
- How can the history and development of such systems be charted and
  assessed?

Although Americans ask some of these questions every day, we
have never had to confront them all at once. The lessons that will
emerge in the great changes in Eastern Europe could, by optimistic
analysis, yield important intelligence about our own media system,
much as the recovery of those nations ravaged in World War II
taught us economic lessons in the 1970s and 1980s.

For this reason I believe there is considerable value in fostering
thoughtful analyses of our media system, especially when it is
compared to others. We Americans have a penchant for idealism
that pushes us to improve, refine, and change what we do and our
way of doing it. Although there is much to be proud of, our present
arrangements in the media system we have and the need to be
responsive to a modern world—yes, an increasingly global one—
demand that we not only celebrate our triumphs and diagnose our
ills but also link those critiques to practical and hard-headed patterns of change.

2. Can News Survive in an Age of Information?[†]

In January 1990, an editorial in the *New York Times* tried to divine the meaning of the 1980s as a prelude to the 1990s. It grappled with such monikers as the "Age of Revolution," referring to Mikhail Gorbachev, Eastern Europe and China; the "Age of Greed," describing the juxtaposition of great fortunes and homeless people; but finally settled on the "Age of Speed" because of the rapid acceleration of information in the last decade as phones and faxes, microchips and personal computers, satellites and cable services, changed the world. It was also an "Age of Convergence," as many forms of communication came together in a single electronically based, computer-driven system. This has most often been called the "Age of Information," a time when a series of evolutionary technological changes affected the fabric of life globally and, in the process, brought us closer together.

Much has been said about the links between the satellite, the television set and the computer, which are present in most places we go or things we do. For the news media, where once the lines between print and broadcast media were clear and unmistakable, convergence meant a blurring and merging. Some observers spoke of a "united state of media" wherein there was no longer much difference between a newspaper, a television station, and an electronic database. All of them gather, process, and distribute information to a consuming public. As media companies—which often call themselves information companies—acquired broadcast stations, cable services, market research firms, outdoor advertising firms, newspapers, magazines and book publishers, their executives increasingly began to speak about information products wherein news was just one of several commodities to be offered to the public.

Nowhere was this more evident than at the national television networks, which historically had developed different divisions for news, entertainment, sports, and other services. Recently those once distinct functions have shifted, sometimes blurring one into the other, or so it seems. For the networks, the news had been something

---

† Lecture given January 9, 1990; Lecture No. 25 in the Press-Enterprise Lecture Series, University of California, Riverside.

of a loss-leader that was not required to make a profit to survive. A different standard had been used to measure Edward R. Murrow and his successors in television news than that applied to prime-time entertainment programs, in which ratings and profits had always been king. In the 1980s, some of the special gloss and protected status of television news rubbed thin, as ratings and profits were expected from all aspects of electronic media operations. Well beyond the headlines and industry gossip, it was clear that convergence of ownership was also accompanied by a convergence of many media activities, in which news and advertising became more symbiotically linked, news and entertainment intersected, and sometimes also news and opinion intersected—not that they were ever clinically separated, but certainly they once had more distinctive identities.

In a feverish attempt to retain their dominance, particularly in the face of the declining audience share influenced by cable, VCRs, and other competition, the networks and the television industry turned increasingly to technical pyrotechnics and hype and, inevitably, to a blurring of information and entertainment functions. Recreations or simulations of current and historical events, as well as compelling computer graphics and split-screen transmissions, were some of the ways new technologies were employed to bolster ratings.

These seemingly innocuous innovations actually blurred media functions, more often than not with entertainment values taking precedence over news values. In some instances, thoughtless juxtapositions of news in showy graphic formats actually conveyed unintended opinion that impaired credibility. These innovations, along with quasi-historical docudramas and miniseries, and information-oriented talk shows, disturbed and distressed thoughtful observers. The reason: fewer and fewer Americans can distinguish between what is news and what is entertainment.

As a study by The Times-Mirror Company in August 1989 indicated, public perceptions of news and entertainment are blurred. Although most Americans think of the daily soap operas and evening sitcoms and dramas as entertainment, they are not quite sure about "Geraldo," "The Oprah Winfrey Show," "A Current Affair," "The Reporters," "America's Most Wanted," and other popular programs, sometimes called *tabloid TV*. I think this criticism merits attention as we ask what, if any, consequences does this trend have for the future of news?

Fred W. Friendly and other critics have warned that dilution of the news with entertainment values can be detrimental. They mention sensational tabloid television programs that run back-to-back with the evening news and thus risk confusing the public about news/entertainment distinctions. Of course this does not differ much—except in audience size—with supermarket tabloids sold on the same rack with mainstream newspapers and magazines. I doubt that the *National Enquirer* debases the *Los Angeles Times* because they are sometimes sold on the same newsstand. The greater threat in the long run is the incremental impact of profitable news programming that may cause television executives to encourage more entertainment-oriented news.

Although it is easy to identify the sins of television, much of the same blurring and merging of functions also applies to newspapers and newsmagazines. Although the newsmagazines were once champions of "hard news," that is, news of public affairs and economics, they now showcase the heroes of popular culture—rock stars, actors, dancers, and even dogs and cats. They, too, are scrambling for an audience in an increasingly competitive advertising and subscription market, looking perhaps for a new identity. Newspapers have hardly been immune from forces of entertainment, ratings and packaging. Throughout the 1970s and 1980s, American newspapers engaged in what I have elsewhere called *creative damage control* as they worried about extinction. The result was special sections, more color, more "soft news" about fashion, food, and pop psychology, as well as other features aimed at capturing the "youth market" or "upscale readers."

The problem goes beyond mainstream media competing among themselves, and now includes other vendors who are selling information. Back in colonial times, broadsides, newsletters, and newspapers were about the only public sources of vital news of that era, reporting on ship movements and markets, town meetings, and taxes. But now there are other competitors actively selling or brokering information. An American Express advertisement puts it plainly:

> Our product is information . . . that charges airline tickets, hotel rooms, dining out, the newest fashions and even figures mailing costs for a travel magazine; information that grows money funds, buys and sells equities and manages mergers; information that pays life insurance annuities, figures pricing for collision coverage and creates and pays

mortgages . . . information that schedules entertainment on cable television and electronically guards houses; information that changes kroners into guilders, figures tax rates in Bermuda and helps put financing together for the ebb and flow of world trade.

"American Express," writes communications scholar Dan Schiller, "is not unique. Companies engaged in information-intensive services in banking, communications, data processing, advertising, law, and so on play an ever more critical role in U.S. investment, employment, and international trade." What we have seen develop in the 1980s is a large business information enterprise that will grow to $12 billion in revenues by the year 1992. This is only the tip of the iceberg, as Ma Bell and other vendors get into the information business. Once Will Rogers mused, "All I know is what I read in the papers." Perhaps this could even be said seriously in the 1930s, but certainly not in the 1980s or 1990s, when information comes from many sources and usually at a price.

There is an unfortunate tendency to link information and news together so that it is difficult to distinguish them, making it all the harder for us to fully understand, appreciate or comprehend our news media—especially newspapers and television, the two dominant instruments of public communication. For that, scholars who take the long view can help. The great social scientist Harold Lasswell told us that, functionally, the media engage in surveillance of the environment, correlation of the parts of society, and transmission of the social heritage from one generation to another. A tall order, and one done by informing, influencing, entertaining, and providing a marketplace for goods and services.

We ought to remember that a news story, an editorial, and the crossword puzzle render different intelligence and represent different functions. Although both information and news are in, Harlan Cleveland's words, "renewable resources," they are also commodities for sale, but they are different in degree. Information is the raw material on which news is based. It includes facts, numbers, data, observations, sometimes ordered and organized, sometimes not. Pure information is often cold and clinical—such as weather reports, sports scores, directions, and lists. In Walter Lippmann's formulation, "news is not a mirror of social conditions, but the report of an aspect that has obtruded itself. The news does not tell you how the seed is germinating in the ground, but it may tell you when the first sprout breaks through the surface. It may even tell you what somebody says is happening to the seed underground. It may tell you that the sprout did not come up at the time it was expected. The more points at which any happening can be fixed, objectified, measured, named, the more points there are at which news can occur."

The news as we know it, of course, is a report, and a report is generated by people—professional people who gather information, write stories, edit and transmit them to the public. This is the value-added aspect of news that can be distinguished from the pure information of lists and tables. Whether people generally recognize and appreciate this is another question, however. We must ask whether the demand for news is being largely satisfied by information received over the telephone, through word of mouth, electronic mail, or other instruments in this age of speed and accelerating information. The yield from this question may be an important indicator for newspeople trying to determine what should be included in news reports, what not. As telephone companies are poised to provide electronic yellow pages, something the courts once forbade, the public will have more and more sources of information to answer its questions about daily life—and, at least for upscale audiences, the electronic wherewithal to ask questions like "What will the weather be tomorrow?" "Where did that stock end up on the exchange yesterday?" or "What was the score of that game?"

If our information needs can be satisfied by business information and other sources free and paid, why should we worry about the future of the news media? Will they not simply factor in these new information brokers and offer an expanded range of new topics and arenas of coverage? The answer is no. Information economists have demonstrated that people will spend only a fixed amount of discretionary income on information and entertainment. Certainly the new information brokers will severely challenge newspapers and television as well as magazines. Remember that the new information (as opposed to news) media can reach us by television screens, personal computers, telephone, or mail. Public communication in the United States is largely driven by user fees (subscriptions) and advertising. Clearly this is a finite and limited source.

The main characteristic of the Information Age has been the proliferation of information and information sources, ranging from the limited reach of individual desktop publishing ventures to the overpowering influence of giant media companies, many of them with global interests and aspirations. In this bombardment of more information than we can possibly consume, we see thousands of magazines and newsletters come and go, electronic data services getting a new foothold, and scores of cable channels competing with traditional broadcasters. There is continuous buying and selling of these properties as media entrepreneurs pitch their wares to a public that can only consume so much. In the inevitable shakeout that will come in the 1990s, there is no doubt that traditional media, especially those that deliver the news, will face severe threats to their survival.

All this depends on the public, whether it gets sustenance and satisfaction from news as opposed to other information sources that could challenge the present information order, now led by newspapers and television. Thus I think that newspapers and television news need to become more thoughtful sense-makers for their local communities, regionally or nationally, in whatever market is appropriate. This means thinking about and attending to the audience in a much more thoughtful, creative, and calibrated way than they presently do.

If producing news shows and editing newspapers has been somewhat hit and miss, essentially intuitive in the past, it cannot be in the future. We already have the tools of market research, which alone and unguided by editorial values can put news decisions in the hands of accountants. But read thoughtfully, as a strategic guide to news coverage and follow up, research can give cues about the value of vivid language, graphic illustrations and subject matter that really serve the needs of the reader and viewer.

In the 1990s, this will mean paying close attention to our changing demographics. According to *American Demographics* magazine, there will be increasing ethnic and racial diversity, a resurgence of metropolitan growth, more households with fewer people in them, a spurt upward in household income, more older people, more women in the work force, and many other indicators of profound change in the composition of our country and its citizens. Our communities will become increasingly international. In such a world the news has a place—an important one—but probably only if it makes its voice heard above its information competitors.

The news (and information) delivered by competent news professionals must be in a form that respects the inherent intelligence of the viewer and reader. It must not be laden with meaningless buzz words nor be overly simplistic or incomplete, leaving more questions than it answers. Although modern hypertechnology can answer questions and assemble information, neither it nor any business information service or electronic database can provide interpretative reporting that tells stories, analyzes issues and projects consequences with vivid language and pertinent illustrations. Neither can it offer coherent opinion in the orchestrated fashion of the newspaper editorial and op-ed pages.

Though the often tepid editorial pages of the country do not always have many readers, they can restore their purpose and vitality by restoring the art of passionate prose. In the process they can help readers form opinions about public issues. The opinion sections of newspapers, as well as columnists of all kinds, are what give personality and local identity to a news organization. In doing so, opinion sections can build a loyal following that is confident it has received credible commentary that is both useful and pertinent.

Unfortunately, though, while television has created some superb formats and interpretations for news, it has not yet created a comfortable vehicle for opinion, at least not in a way that effectively showcases different points of view. There are, of course, the well-known Sunday morning public affairs shows, but television still has no effective means of direct viewer feedback, as do the print media's letters-to-the-editor and guest columns. Electronic opinion programs may be just over the horizon, however, as various notions about interactive television come into the economic marketplace.

At a time when every person can be an editor (thanks to databases and other information services), people need to know and understand what it is they are not getting. What they are not getting in information are the values the news media bring. Values that give greater attention to one issue over another because it is more important to more people. I also mean values that distinguish the significant from the trivial; values that deliver ordered, quality news rather than aimless quantities of information. It is clear that the news media do not have an exclusive franchise on information. Much valuable information comes to us from the new media sources mentioned earlier as well as the entertainment media, particularly television and motion pictures. Who is to say that a television program like "L.A. Law" does not convey more information about lawyers than, say, a newspaper series on law firms? There is much information in entertainment programming, and even the crossword puzzle has been known to teach readers a thing or two. But remember, here information is only incidental, not central. The essential difference between news and information is that news is gathered, processed, and presented to the public with agreed-upon professional standards, checked for accuracy, and put in an overall context. Although information is the raw material from which news-people fashion reports, reporters add comments about what these facts or events or processes mean. They find intelligent, well-sourced speculation about what the information means to individual citizens or to institutions. If news is to survive in the Age of Information, we must take some precautions to see that it does, namely:

1. Encourage news organizations to be more forthcoming with information about themselves, until their readers and viewers know what their values are, what standards they operate by, who their staff members are, and why we should trust them and respect their work. It is time to have more visible news staffs with news organizations—even newspapers—giving their audiences a more detailed preview of news coverage, both present and future.

2. Use recent census information to tell local news consumers how coverage will change and why in light of changing demographics. The media need to say to their respective communities, "We know who you are, we are trying to serve you more effectively, and here is how."

3. We need more effective means of public feedback than litigation—approaches that do not impair anyone's freedom of expression. Such means could include ethical audits linking media people and citizens, more open channels for citizen complaint and feedback, possibly local press councils and databases wherein people's concerns can be gathered together, codified and made openly available to the public. In the 1980s, after a major credibility crisis and an explosion of libel litigation, the press settled back once again into what some have called a "public be damned" posture, often arrogantly unresponsive to simple issues of access and understandability, and not always caring whether their readers, viewers, and sources are accorded courtesy and respect. In the name of our collective democratic governance and the media's economic well-being, this must end. The news media need to project a friendly, caring face, saying to their respective constituencies, "We care about you and we are open to your concerns."

4. It would also be a public service for the press to promote its own professionalism in overt fashion, explaining how a particular story was developed, what ethical issues were involved and how they were resolved. An interactive approach to this process would be even more effective.

5. The news media should confront a very difficult, but not insolvable problem: that of defining the public interest. It is common to claim

allegiance to "the public interest," but when asked to define it we say lazily, "That's impossible." I believe it is possible; that the concept of the public interest, linked closely with the ancient idea of *vox populi*, can be thought through, explicated, discussed, and debated. We have for too long confused what is *of* public interest—matters sensational or simple morbid curiosity—with what is *in* the public interest. Philosophers, ethicists, legal scholars, members of the clergy, and others have addressed these issues, and though there is no universally accepted formulation, there is a rich yield of thought that can help all of us think through the idea of the public interest—whether it is a fusion of many special interests and self-serving pleas or a more abstract and generalized concept. We could then relate the idea to local issues, controversies, trends and enduring public questions. While there may be no mechanical test for the public interest, it is an idea too important to be written off with an arrogant wave of the arm. It requires the kind of hard thought of which citizens and their communicators are capable.

If the media return to their essential public service function, distinguishing news from information, linking news and opinion but maintaining some orderly separation, we will better understand that news embraces information, but with value added: the commitment of sensitive editors and caring publishers and broadcasters who realize the essence of their public franchise and who seek to distinguish themselves from other businesses by fostering public trust in the service of the public interest.

Just because we do not all agree what the public interest is at any given time is not a reason to forsake the ideal. Doing so could lead the news media to succumb to information services. That would be a loss for us all, because in opting for easy access to information, some of us will not know what to ask for, others will not be able to afford it, and still others leading understandably busy lives will miss the richness and texture only news can offer. In the end our democratic system is well served by news rigorously acquired and presented that guides, instructs, and gives us the kind of ordered information capital we need to keep freedom of expression well and strong.

3. News, Ethics, and Split-Personality Journalism[†]

When we look at the condition of American journalism today it is sometimes difficult to tell whether the extraordinary changes brought about by the convergence of new technologies, which allows for faster and more efficient newsgathering, processing, and dissemination, is elevating or debasing journalistic quality.

In my job at the Gannett Center for Media Studies, I am frequently asked to comment on the state of journalism, usually in connection with some controversy. These inquiries from television correspondents, magazine writers, and newspaper reporters are concerned with everything from coverage of politics to the ethics of particular news organizations and even particular news people. I have been asked to comment, for example, on the role of network anchors, the Andy Rooney affair, the tabloid tale of the Trumps, and many other topics. Often the questions from media critics and reporters are connected to technology and the changes that have come to American media, especially in the 1980s.

This has been a time when the economics of communication have shifted markedly, growing ever more global and giant; when ownerships have changed and concentration has accelerated; when hundreds of new outlets—some of them cable channels, others magazines and newspapers—have expanded people's options for information and news. All this was spurred by the satellite, the computer and other devices that gave us instantaneous live news from most points on the globe. Along with new electronic databases, computer graphics, and the beginnings of artificial intelligence, both the look and the nature of the news are changing.

Those who carefully track these changes make one of two conclusions, and it is easy to see why: Some say that journalism is in decline, while others say it is improving, causing us to ask whether journalism indeed has a split personality. Let us examine these two propositions.

---

† Speech given at the Ninth Carol Burnett Fund Lecture on Ethics in Journalism, "In Allegiance to the Truth: News, Ethics, and Split Personality Journalism," March 6, 1990, Department of Journalism, University of Hawaii, Honolulu.

First, journalism is in decline. In February 1990 the world was treated to the battle of the Trumps, wherein the marital squabbling of America's tycoon of the moment, Donald Trump, a flamboyant, publicity-seeking billionaire, and his equally avaricious wife Ivana, pushed Nelson Mandela, Eastern Europe, Central America, and the heavyweight boxing championship of the world off the front pages of the tabloids and consumed both time and space in our most respectable newspapers, magazines, and television programs. This exhibitionistic performance by the tabloids, which spread to other media, came on the heals of the expansion of so-called tabloid television, which makes it difficult for viewers to distinguish news from entertainment. The Trump affair, many critics argued, was news coverage run amok—news that trivialized our world and debased other more important matters. But what caused it to happen in the first place, especially in the face of such important competing news?

I believe it was, in part at least, technology. In many respects tabloid newspapers—the kind with big, blotchy headlines that scream out from the newsstand—are a thing of the past. Except for the supermarket tabloids, most big-city "scandal sheets" are artifacts of another generation. They were initially born in a period of great newspaper competition, and though that time has passed, the great expansion in television and cable programs has brought back keen competition for readers, viewers, and advertising dollars. This is especially true for television news, where the four broadcast networks and an increasing number of sensational tabloid television shows such as "Geraldo," "A Current Affair," "The Reporters," "America's Most Wanted" and others are competing fiercely for essentially the same audience.

In the midst of this intense battle are the last remaining big-city tabloids. The New York *Daily News, New York Post, New York Newsday,* the *Boston Herald*, and a few others are trying to survive in a market where large numbers of attentive consumers are best achieved in television, not print media. In their scramble to outdo local television news and tabloid television, columnists and editors at these papers seized on the Trump story and played it for all it was worth and more. And as a story it worked. It was a perfect formula to foster sensationalism. We had celebrity, wealth, power, sex, a love triangle, even religion, and Valentine's Day. This exhibitionistic explosion might have been limited mostly to New York audiences if it had not been for a vitriolic battle between syndicated columnists, the clash of high-profile media consultants, and other "players" who, for a few days, made this both a national and international story.

The extraordinary competition represented in the coverage of the Trump affair was linked to new technical devices that more accurately measure television viewing (the people meters) and have for the first time calibrated the important role of cable, VCRs, and other competitive media that are pushing newspapers and newsmagazines in new directions. Too often that means away from the hard news of economics, government, and the environment and toward human interest and gossip.

Technology has also been a culprit in more direct ways, evidenced by two examples in 1989. First, there was the dramatic report on "ABC World News Tonight," wherein viewers were treated to some remarkably grainy footage showing an American diplomat passing secrets to the Soviets. There was only one thing wrong: The pictures were a deliberate deception, a video "re-creation." Those depicted were not diplomats and spies, but ABC staff role-playing. More importantly, perhaps, the *story was based on allegations*, not proven facts.

This incident and subsequent simulations of news events, historical scenes and even projections of the future became something of a media cause célèbre for several months before most of the networks decided to ban their use. Such re-creations are still common, however, on some of the tabloid television programs and severely confuse viewers who are trying to distinguish fact from fiction. Not incidentally, dramatic re-creations were long ago defended by press lord Henry Luce as "fakery in allegiance to the truth."

There is nothing inherently wrong with the wonderful technological devices that bring us dramatic re-creations—it is the *way* they are presented that misleads the public and impairs media credibility. In fact, a study commissioned by the Times Mirror Company in 1989 found that a substantial number of Americans could not definitively judge whether some television programs were news or entertainment.

The other regrettable, technology-aided judgment of 1989 was the networks' use of a split screen in their coverage of the U.S. invasion of Panama. On one side of the screen were flag-draped coffins of American soldiers killed in Panama and on the other a jocular press conference with President Bush. The visual effect was what one critic called a "split personality": There was little direct relationship between the two pictures and the president did not know that his press conference was being juxtaposed with the unloading of caskets. Here the split screen, which originally came to us in sports coverage, was so thoughtlessly used as to make both the president and the media look bad. It did nothing to advance news coverage, although it could have.

But beyond these two examples is ample evidence that news coverage is not declining or suffering at all. Thus the proposition that *journalism is improving*.

We can contrast the negative effects of misused technology with some important and impressive coverage in a year when the news media seemed to celebrate one of their finest hours. Correspondents and anchors captured the turmoil in Tiananmen Square, the collapse of the Berlin Wall and the great changes—subtle and violent—in the Soviet Union and Eastern Europe. At the same time critical activities in Central America and South Africa also captured our attention. And quick, accurate reporting gave us stunning coverage of Hurricane Hugo and the 1989 San Francisco earthquake. The same media that brought us these matters of great (and probably lasting) moment, also gave us news of drugs and crime, as well as the environment, government and the economy. Even the harshest critics of the press agreed that this was a laudable performance in a year that may go down as seminal in the history of Western civilization.

And here the principal catalyst to comprehending these events was technology. Tiny, lightweight cameras and easy satellite uplinks took viewers to the scene of great world events as they happened, even if they did exhaust our valiant, globe-trotting network anchors. The superb coverage of the Philippine revolution, for example, occurred when electronic newsgathering (ENG) was just celebrating its 10th anniversary. At the Gannett Center we conducted a demonstration contrasting news from the Philippines a decade earlier with the events that led to the downfall of Ferdinand Marcos. The revolution that deposed Marcos was covered live from the scene, a story that developed minute by minute, visually and dramatically unfolding in living color. Only a decade before, broadcast news had relied heavily on still, black-and-white photographs supplied by the Associated Press. One can only imagine the effects of these stark contrasts on what people know, understand, and feel about the great news events of today.

Juxtaposed against these two divergent appraisals of our media is the continuing worry that journalistic performance is necessarily influenced by the forces of globalism and giantism that are swallowing up our media system and those of other countries. News organizations that are a part of big business are governed by market forces, and market research is said to determine what America (and the rest of the world) reads, hears, and watches.

Thus, we readers and viewers are hearing contradictory things about our media. We hear that news coverage is out of control, witnessing the Trump affair or dramatic re-creations. People who follow these arguments and observe news coverage that is based on the musings of gossip columnists, rumor, and deliberate deception might conclude there is little quality control in the information reaching us.

On the other hand, there are the extraordinary performances by journalists covering more of the globe than ever before, such as both Tom Brokaw's and Peter Jennings's reportage of world events in 1989-1990. And considering the human and financial resources invested for the *New York Times* and other media organizations to deliver what may well be the best performance on a story that I have seen in my lifetime—that of Eastern Europe and the Soviet Bloc—the case is easily made that American journalism is getting better all the time.

No matter which interpretation of the news best fits our needs and biases, most of us agree that what we really want is "the truth," however illusory that notion is. Still, we are confronted by economic movements on Wall Street and those in boardrooms around the world who think of the media mostly as machines producing widgets. We are told by some critics that the media more than ever are driven by the greed of a market that values short-run profits over long-term investments. The results for networks and national newsmagazines, we are told, are shrinking staffs and depleted resources. The audience numbers that generate advertising revenues drive news organizations and, in a circular fashion, cause them to court audiences to whom their advertisers can sell their products and services. In a system of communication paid for by only two revenue streams—user fees and advertising—how could it be otherwise? Information is for sale to the highest bidder, and the media have organized themselves to court upscale audiences, paying little or no attention to the underclass and other unattractive and—by market definition—dispossessed communities.

A close examination of the media world today, as well as the role news plays in it, is a view of great fragmentation. With scores of cable channels, thousands of magazines and other rapidly fragmenting media, it is clear that virtually every interest and every point of view, no matter how narrow, is being served. At the same time traditional media such as newspapers and television are challenged by the pressures of the new media and find it increasingly difficult to serve "the whole community." Instead they serve the "audience" of readers and viewers who actually subscribe, pay cable fees, or loyally watch television news. We must continually ask whether the fragmentation that enhances freedom of expression to smaller and smaller communities of interest also promotes the kind of freedom that bonds a nation together. We have not yet begun to ask these questions with clarity, let alone find methods for answering them rigorously and accurately.

Perhaps we need a national endowment to preserve the news—not a government agency or even a political mandate—but a commitment by our news organizations to do more than business as usual, to engage in a national commitment to quality news in a manner that instructs us all about: (a) the operative theory of journalism by which any given news organization guides itself; (b) the resources it has devoted to newsgathering; (c) the ways in which the public ought to assess and evaluate the results; and finally, (d) how individual readers and viewers might "talk back" to or interact with news editors and producers.

Although I believe that the diversity that brings us Trumpian headlines in the tabloids also brings us serious analysis on the editorial page, we lack serious understanding of our current "theory" of journalism. Journalists hate the word *theory*, but it is the best word I know to describe those commitments, values, and organizing principles that explain what they are doing.

Years ago our operative theory in American journalism was "objectivity," also known as "the Jack Webb school of journalism" and consisted of a "just the facts, ma'am" approach to balancing "both sides" of a controversy. I was one of many writers and critics beginning in the late 1960s who strongly opposed this simple-minded approach to journalism in an increasingly ambiguous world in which there are seemingly 16 sides to every controversy, not just two. Objectivity was also a theory of journalism that almost always valued official sources over ordinary people. In 1971 I wrote that "the increasing complexity of public affairs made it difficult to confine reporting to the strait-jacket of unelaborated fact" (Dennis & Rivers, 1971)

Although editors initially rejected the many assaults on objectivity, it was not long before they, too, retreated from the concept and began to talk about "fairness," which was a vague, fuzzy and somewhat more comfortable euphemism for objectivity, with some complex twists. Unfortunately, in rejecting good old-fashioned objectivity we really did not replace it with any alternative model, and partly as a consequence many in the public are confused about news coverage that gives the same value to the Trump affair as it does to the release of Nelson Mandela.

I believe that we ought to return to a new interpretative objectivity in which central facts can be verified but in which matters of interpretation and analysis are identified as such and left to reader and viewer discretion. There are descriptive details and facts that can be sorted out and identified in virtually every news situation, ranging from a simple police matter to a complex international controversy. Events arise, people are involved, and situations can be observed. This is and ought to be descriptive, verified journalism at its best.

I would pair this kind of descriptive journalism, which would be by definition as impartial as possible, with the yield of modern computer-assisted reporting and database retrieval. We have better and more systematic tools than ever before and can assemble more facts more efficiently, thus greatly enhancing our reporting. Here again, technology can be an aid to reporting rather than a hindrance to understanding.

At the same time, we need to pair descriptive journalism with more interpretative and analytic work that tells us what the various forces and vested interests are in connection with a news story. Sometimes, when the media perform particularly poorly, as they did in their late and labored coverage of AIDS, they need to publicly fess up to missed cues, bias, and less than exemplary coverage. The nation's major media picked up the AIDS story long after it had evolved, and then only because of personal factors, not any sense of objective reality. This sad chapter in American journalism is documented in James Kinsella's book *Covering the Plague: AIDS and the American Media*. In large part the story was ignored because editors believed it affected unattractive and unimportant constituencies. Only after the Rock Hudson revelations and other instances in which individual journalists' families were involved did the press

begin with any seriousness to cover this critical public health problem. Some critics believe the press should shoulder some of the
blame for the spread of the disease because of a kind of de facto
censorship that deprived the American people of important information. When subsequent coverage—much of it superb—did gain
momentum, health practices improved markedly.

The AIDS story demonstrated the hypocrisy of the journalistic
fairness argument. Not only was a major public health story under-
played or missed entirely for years but it also gained notoriety only
when there were personal stakes for reporters and editors. This was
not impartial journalism, nor was it in any sense fair.

It seems to me that such a new interpretative objectivity would
be enhanced if our media organizations—without being overly
self-conscious—told us more about their methods. How are major
stories being covered and with what staffing—both in numbers and
with attention to the backgrounds and interests of reporters? In a
good deal of international coverage we have had reporters with
mixed experience, knowledge, credentials, and dedication to impartial reports. Many will readily admit their ideological preferences,
some of which are hardly conducive to impartial reporting.

Leaders of media organizations would help their own cause and
understanding if they would step forward and indicate by what
standard they want to be judged. In a society in which all of us can
be critics and analysts if we wish, it would be helpful to have
straightforward statements from leading editors and broadcast executives indicating just what their goals, purposes, and measures of
quality control are.

In a period when we are increasing our capacity for interactive
television and other two-way systems, our media need to concern
themselves with a better system of public feedback. There are the
superb Times Mirror studies of public perceptions of the news
media, studies that draw important baseline data. But we need more
than that: a chance for readers and viewers to be heard, not one by
one in every editor's office, but possibly through computer inven-
tories of people's concerns and grievances. Some of these will have
to do with access to information and understandability; others will
focus on factual errors or differences of interpretation. Some criti-
cisms will be on target, others will be terribly wrong, but collectively
they will provide better intelligence with which editors and other
media people can determine how well they are doing. This idea is

not to slavishly please readers and viewers but to make certain that news is being presented in a coherent and effective fashion. Readers and viewers might themselves be encouraged to suggest approaches to the public dialogue that would be good for all of us and as well advance freedom of expression.

I believe that, in general, American journalism really is improving. There are occasional egregious slips, sometimes brought on by overzealous use of technology in instances when new tools are used thoughtlessly or in a trivial way. But when used with foresight, as with computer-assisted reporting or electronic newsgathering, news can be presented with more dramatic force and more accuracy, and the result will be a better-informed public. To do that, news people need to plan their work with greater vision and at the same time be willing to explain it in an open manner that may often invite public criticism.

Then, I think, we will have both a freer, more responsive and more vital journalism in America and elsewhere in the world. We might even have a new allegiance to the truth made possible not just by new technological tools and more thoughtful interactive journalism but by mutual respect between speaker and listener, between the media and their audience, that we so sorely need today.

4. Political Insiders and Media Ethics[†]

The sanctity of the journalistic temple is under scrutiny once again.

At issue is the proper bounds for journalists in their relationships with politics and government. Although in other countries the line between public life and coverage of public life is often blurred, even nonexistent, we in the United States have frowned on that—in recent years, at least—holding it a journalistic article of faith that media organizations ought to report on, analyze, and give opinions about government but not participate directly in the process of governing. Indeed we talk of an adversarial relationship between press and government.

---

† *Communiqué* column, February 1989 (monthly newsletter of FFMSC).

Washington Post columnist David Broder warns of the dangers inherent in blurring the line between politicians and journalists. He worries that some journalists could become "androgynous Washington insiders" seeking and wielding inappropriate influence. When journalists become insiders, Broder argues, they damage journalistic independence and impair public trust.

In an angry response Patrick Buchanan disagrees, arguing that rather than becoming "unauthentic" by virtue of their government service and special access, journalists end up serving the public in a more knowledgeable way.

Despite their sharp disagreement, both have a point. In an ideal world the reporter, analyst, and critic make intelligent and impartial judgments. Education and experience, whether in journalism, government, or other fields, can be enormously advantageous.

But the role and function of government on the one hand and the press on the other are discretely different. The confusion comes when news organizations employ government insiders as commentators and critics, people who offer interpretations not as journalists but as former public servants. They are not simply sources integrated into a news story or broadcast, but paid employees whose roles are often blurred in the public mind with those of the journalist.

The columnist who coaches a presidential candidate and then covers a presidential debate, the editor who advises a president and editorializes on the president's handling of the very issue under discussion without revealing his insider status, cross the line and violate public trust.

Ironically, though, we seem never to have a problem with media owners and high-level executives mixing government service with the running of communications enterprises. There are cases in which those active in the media have taken political roles, even served in office.

Set against the purist view of the insider issue is the widely recognized fact that the media institutionally are no longer innocent bystanders in the process of governing—if they ever were. Their influence comes from the selection of news and commentary that help determine what the public thinks is important. No one seems to ask the hard question as to whether an institution that is so central to politics and government, one that might actually set the public agenda, can, in fact, have employees who as individuals stand outside that web of influence. To the extent that there is a revolving door between government and the press, it is important for the ethics of media organizations to be clearly stated and understood. People who recently served in government probably should not be assessing the performance of their successors as columnists and commentators, at least not without a decent interval. And in their maiden columns they ought to declare their independence from previous employers, whether in government and politics or the private sector.

The important question for the public is: What standards of professionalism, if any, does the press live by? There are many kinds of journalists, but all of them, I believe, want to enjoy the public's trust. That can only happen when people who gather, write, and edit the news make it clear that their first responsibility is to accurate information honorably gathered.

There will always be insiders, some who enjoy the one-upmanship of information gathered from intimate contacts, others who flaunt relationships that blur connections with professional responsibility. The best of these people are open about the nature of their sources, if not the sources themselves. And when they are not, others often prod their memoirs about conflict of interest.

It is good that David Broder opened this debate. The dilemma he sees has few easy answers, but it comes at a time when ethics in government are under increasing scrutiny.

5. Fakery in Allegiance to the Truth[†]

Allegations in October 1989 that CBS News allowed faked footage of the Afghanistan war to pass through its usually well-screened evening news was a jolt to many Americans who rely on television news for accurate reports of the world beyond their grasp.

If the news media have one redeeming feature with the public, it is that they are believable and credible. Although a few news reports with deceptive visualizations will not seriously undermine our reliance on

---

† *Communiqué* column, October 1989 (monthly newsletter of FFMSC).

our ubiquitous media, the possibility that a few particularly egregious deceptions could do so is disturbing.

At the same time there was a lively discussion of "re-creations" or "simulations" in which television producers stage an event or scene to illustrate the news. Sometimes such staged events are effective historical recreation, clearly labeled and presented as such. There is nothing new about this device: such re-creations were the stock-in-trade of some of the best of the early documentary film-makers and, as well, the 1940s' "March of Time," which in both its radio and film incarnations used actors to reenact events. Henry Luce called the style "fakery in allegiance to the truth."

Re-creations such as the one ABC News did in reports on accused diplomat Felix Bloch, on the other hand, are deliberate deceptions. Other re-creations of the type employed by the syndicated "whodunit" shows—murders, robberies, kidnappings, and so on—are not deliberately deceitful but nonetheless come perilously close to the line.

Typically, re-creations are not intended to mislead but to provide richer visual material to illustrate the story. This is not much different than the scene-setting done by magazine writers as they re-create scenes they themselves did not witness, but establish through reliable witnesses.

Although the controversy in 1989 was directed toward CBS News, the larger issue is control of the camera and reliable supervision by professional journalists of their news product. Although the media have used free-lance writers and photographers for generations, we now see more and more free-lance and commissioned news footage on television news because modern technology allows almost anyone with a video camera to produce it. At many local television stations, newshounds, some of them teenagers, carry such footage to newspeople and offer it for sale. Sometimes newspeople even encourage it in an effort to involve the public in the newsgathering process, to get unusual material and to boost ratings.

This is obviously fraught with risk. The news organization must check and verify the material it buys, as well as the reliability of the people who provide it. If this is done effectively, there is nothing wrong with letting the public join in the process of gathering news and information. In fact, it is a wonderfully democratic notion, adding diversity to our news accounts much as "country correspondents," amateurs all, did for newspapers from the eighteenth century forward.

It should be noted that anyone, even the most rigorous news organization, can at times be fooled. The *New York Times Magazine* once published a story supposedly written in Cambodia by a resourceful free-lance writer who falsely claimed to be providing an eyewitness account of his topic. In this instance the writer even managed to have his copy sent in envelopes postmarked in Cambodia.

The CBS affair should not be used to excoriate free-lance writers or those with an eye for news who feel compelled to record and capture events. The intention of those gathering information, their competence, and the conditions of the newsgathering, however, should be carefully investigated. Self-serving individuals and groups could easily fake, distort, or mislead the public with very convincing video or written material.

Because we do not and should not license journalists, we live in a society in which everyone can communicate using modern technological tools. That is a good thing, and a few misfires should not lead us to cut off such a useful and natural impulse. However, news organizations now need to be more vigilant than ever in their efforts to provide sound information. Their reputation and our intelligence about the world depend on it.

PART II

On International Communication

6. Reporting the News From Abroad[†]

In a year when international affairs have commanded so much media attention in the United States and elsewhere, it is useful to consider the role of the foreign correspondent, a term itself dated in an era of interdependence.

From the earliest times, news from abroad prepared by our own press corps has captivated our imagination. A cursory look at international correspondence conjures up images of swashbuckling reporters like Richard Harding Davis traveling continents in search of adventure, or others standing at history's precipice. Only recently, the wartime journalism of William L. Shirer was the subject of a television series that captured his observations from Nazi Germany in the years before World War II.

Reporting from abroad, whether for television, newspapers, or magazines, is still one of the most prestigious and highly valued assignments in American journalism. Such experience often plays a role in journalists' ascension to major editorships or anchor positions.

Much has been written by and about foreign correspondents, and the image that emerges from that literature is intriguing and contradictory. Much of it is highly sophisticated, in that the best of foreign correspondents are erudite and educated.

Some years ago, however, critics complained that our overseas press corps was not very sophisticated, not well trained in languages or foreign cultures. In some cases this is still true, but rarely. Although the number of foreign correspondents has continued to decline and the amount of foreign news in American media has diminished, knowledgeable observers speak admiringly of foreign correspondents, not just for their knowledge and ability to traverse a "foreign" land but also for their wherewithal psychologically to function on their own away from the office and the culture of journalism itself.

---

† *Communiqué* column, November 1989 (monthly newsletter of FFMSC).

If there is something contradictory about the advance of foreign correspondence since the days of Richard Halliburton, who sometimes fabricated stories, it is that while reporters' facility with the subjects they cover has advanced mightily, journalism itself has not. Most international coverage is exactly how Mort Rosenblum of the Associated Press describes it in his book, *Coups and Earthquakes*: event-oriented, tied to crises, catastrophes, political happenings, and matters quite overt. It rarely integrates information from other fields or pays attention to process-oriented topics like international economics, environmental change, or world health.

In many ways international correspondence is a glossy version of old-fashioned saloon reporting, a primitive form of journalism that seems untouched by the reforms in style and epistemology that have occurred in domestic journalism since the 1960s. The reporter covering city hall in a small community is usually armed with some concern about impartiality, about sorting out the main players and issues, about linking these to audience interests, and finally, in summing up, in making sense.

All too many foreign correspondents, steeped in the politics and lore of a given country, bring an ideological bias to their work. It is especially disturbing to read that some foreign correspondents approach their assignment with so much knowledge of their subject but so little philosophical commitment to reporting itself. It has often been said that many reporters have no "theory," no commitment to organizing principles that lead to coherent work or link it to previous coverage.

Thus the yield of much foreign correspondence appears self-conscious, muddled or biased. Rarely does a clear picture emerge, one that moves beyond surface events into the process of news. And rarely is the journalism itself advanced in structure, form or style.

This is regrettable because some of our most able journalistic talents come to see themselves not so much as reporters and observers but as foreign policy experts, writing not for the public at large but for policymakers in Washington and elsewhere.

The media community needs to pay serious attention to this evident deficiency. What is needed is more intellectual leadership from our distinguished correspondents abroad.

7. News and the New World Order[†]

As the world lurched and churned in the first year of the decade of the 1990s, it was evident that changes in alignments and attitudes were more than incremental. These changes, it seems, are profound enough to cause people to consider whether we are witnessing the beginnings of a new world order.

For the news media, especially the American media, the world available for coverage has largely been defined by crisis and conflict. Any continuity in international reporting has been driven by concern that important international arrangements, regions, and countries warrant adequate treatment. Thoughtful commentators always maintained that for the public to be fully informed some kind of representative coverage of the "whole world" was necessary.

But what was the whole world? Seen through the prism of Western coverage, it usually amounted to capitals and countries where the United States or its allies had foreign policy interests. Some nations and leaders were simply deemed more important than others due to economic and military influence, ethnic factors or, in some cases, prestige based on a moral position.

The boundaries of the world order for the media were not very complicated. There was first and foremost the Western alliance. Next we looked to our adversaries, typically the Soviet Union and the Warsaw Pact countries. There was always the developing world, the so-called Third World of Latin America, Africa, and Asia. An overarching consideration was the persistent strain of the Cold War, which not only pitted the United States and its allies against the Soviet Union and its satellites but also reverberated to other parts of the world where countries were seen as client states, either manipulating or being manipulated by the major powers.

Like it or not, the world media learned the rules of the game, and our respective views of the world, and each other, were well understood. From time to time there was the flicker of change, usually influenced by a crisis, wherein a country long out of our gaze would appear center stage for a short time before again exiting.

† FFMSC Conference Report, "News and the New World Order," January 21, 1991.

A number of debates have emerged about what is covered and why. In the 1970s and 1980s, there was much talk about what was then called the New World Information and Communication Order, a concept championed by UNESCO, amid much controversy, which pitted the developed world of the West against the emerging nations of Africa and Latin America, for example.

Putting important matters of ideology and journalistic freedom aside for a moment, the central issue of debate was the flow of information that informs the world community and public life. Most agreed that the flow was one way: from the large, industrial nations to the smaller, developing nations. There was, however, much disagreement about the consequences of such conditions. In 1991, as the Cold War apparently ended, news coverage simply has different concerns, different baselines of activity. News now is more often defined not so much by nations, but by economies, by global human forces as well as conditions of nature, as for example the environment. New rules are being written; our concept of what is important has changed and so has the nature and contours of news.

Naturally, this is a good time to think about news in the context of the new world order. News budgets and sensibilities of reporters and editors, as well as their sources and the public, are an indication of the change that is coming.

But there needs to be deeper thinking about the implications of the changes in reporting priorities of recent years, especially as we approach the year 2000. The public is still entitled to a full account of the day's news, but the scope and dimensions of that account are now in play and in need of a clearer definition.

8. Images of the Soviet Union in the United States[†]

It is hard to imagine citizens of any country who are not vitally interested in how their country is portrayed elsewhere in the world. Thus it is especially noteworthy at a time when commentators are proclaiming the end of the Cold War that Soviet images of the United States, and American images of the Soviet Union, should be the concern of an international conference.

Because media portrayals are thought to be closely linked to public opinion and public policy, they are especially important during transitional periods. It is easy to speak glibly about mutual images and to describe them impressionistically without measurement or systematic assessment. All of us know that for each of the two great superpowers the image of the other is shifting, yet we rarely consider the multifaceted nature of the resulting images and what impact, if any, they have on people in the two countries.

Images or representations of people, ideas, and even nations have been part of the literature of media studies for decades. It is fragmented research, however, typically reporting what the manifest content of a given medium has said about a particular topic. In the 1980s, as the beginnings of the end of the Cold War were reported in world media, scholars began to study such topics as the image of the Soviet Union in U.S. television entertainment programs, the nature and shape of news reports on television in the two countries, and such specific topics as comparative summit coverage. The result, as a June-July 1989 Moscow State University conference has reported, is a clearer and better understanding of media images in the two countries.

Some of this emerging research is also concerned with the definition of news in the two countries, the changing nature of journalists, structural control of the media, government regulation, freedom of expression, and other issues. It is generally acknowledged that the Soviet media are changing faster than media institutions in the United States, especially with the introduction and convergence of the

---

† Speech given on June 26, 1989, "Images of the Soviet Union in the United States: An Agenda for Research." Moscow State University.

concepts of *glasnost* and *perestroika*. As important as the Gorbachev
years have been to opening a new era of diplomatic relations between the two countries, the images we have of each other go back
a long way, and their residual imprints on individuals and national
psyches are part of our institutional memories.

Here I wish to consider several aspects of the news media and the
functions the media perform in society. These are important to any
consideration of mutual images. I will also suggest topics and trends
that might be explored by scholars and professionals who want to
better understand and track the American view of the Soviet Union.
Finally, I will link these considerations of content to what we know
about the impact, influence, and effect of media on people, institutions and society. After all, the images we see on television and in
the print press almost always influence thought, sometimes shape
attitudes, and occasionally determine behavior.

The task of connecting content concerns with media effects is
especially pertinent at a time when scholars speak of a so-called
paradigm shift wherein the "power" of the press is being reconsidered. Though once it was thought that media had direct and profound effects, later researchers doubted this and downplayed such
influence. Since the late 1970s, however, students of the media have
joined in what sometimes is called a "return" to a powerful (though
qualified) effects theory. Because media scholars often have an elitist
penchant for serious images emerging from information and news,
they pay less than full attention to the several functions of mass
communication and the various media that fulfill them. Students of
Soviet images in the United States are more likely to direct their
attention to major elite newspapers, the television networks, prime-
time programming, and on occasion, the movies. Most comparative
study involves the news and information functions of the mass
media; images on the pages of major national and regional newspapers, and on network news and wire services, are likely targets for
investigation.

Fortunately this narrow band is expanding as critics and commentators probe all media functions and media organizations. There are
news and information services provided by so-called trash television
programs like "A Current Affair," "The Reporters," and "Geraldo,"
which are watched by millions, not to mention the supermarket
tabloids, such as the *National Enquirer,* with their blotchy headlines
and breathless exposés.

The information media in the United States are also expanding. There are thousands of general-circulation newspapers and mostly specialized magazines, as well as on-line databases. There are house organs, church bulletins, special newsletters, MTV news programs, and news directed only at children or the elderly. The connection between the information function of the media, defined as "pure news," and the opinion function of the media is sometimes fragile. But editorial pages, op-ed columns, television talk shows, talk radio, and commentaries all contribute to opinion-making. Added to news and opinion is the entertainment function of television. Images are built in serious drama, arts programming, situation comedies, sports, variety shows, and other television content, as well as through magazines and other media that entertain. Moreover in a capitalist society no one would seriously dismiss the role of advertising, which casts a long shadow in image creation.

In each of the four functional areas of mass communication— news, opinion, entertainment, and advertising—there are many different kinds of media with different purposes and most of them offer consumers differing portrayals of the Soviet Union. On the same evening that Americans were moved by Tom Brokaw's historic interview with Mikhail Gorbachev, they also may have watched commercials that portrayed Soviets as buffoons and prime-time entertainment fare crawling with conniving KGB agents.

In still another arena there were lingering images of great Soviet athletes competing in international sports and Soviet dance companies touring the United States and displaying their art on public television. These are only a few of the flickering images of the Soviet Union in the United States.

Clearly, any consideration of images must be aware of how necessarily complex and multifaceted this inquiry must be. Similarly, if Soviet or U.S. citizens concerned with better relations between the two countries are put off by the wide range of U.S. media images, it is well to remember that the United States, while increasingly internationally minded, still erects barriers to easy international understanding. For much of our history we were essentially an isolationist country, having thrown off the yoke of Britain and decrying "foreign entanglements." Indeed, this was the warning of George Washington in his farewell address. Add to this the unyielding mandate of the Monroe Doctrine, which bars foreign powers from the Americas, and the backdrop of mutual relations is more coherent. Until recently, rather than celebrate ethnic diversity in America, we were more likely to insist on Americanization, assuming that anyone who would become a citizen should speak English and cherish traditions dating back to the revolution. Also, until recently, we have insisted on "language purity," which means "English only."

So great is our parochialism in the United States that international visitors are sometimes surprised, even astonished by it. "How can a country so well-known and admired elsewhere in the world be so blind to others on this planet?" critics sometimes ask. I recall a French scholar visiting the United States expressing exasperation over the paucity of news from his native France in the *Minneapolis Tribune,* the paper in the town where he was staying. In a three-month period, he said, there was a single story published about France and that was a one-inch item on the decline of beret production! When he confronted the local newspaper editor, he was told, "We don't edit this paper for visiting Frenchmen."

Thus U.S. media filter news and information (as well as other images) of the rest of the world in a fashion that they believe will be responsive to their audiences' interests. Television viewers and newspaper readers are thought not to want encyclopedic coverage of France, the Soviet Union, or any other country unless such coverage is especially pertinent and salient to them.

This issue—what makes information, opinion, entertainment, and marketing images of interest locally—should be the topic of another inquiry. For most of the American media, it is thought that information and images from abroad often follow foreign policy or great world events. Although sometimes a scientific discovery, such as the discovery of King Tutankhamen's tomb in 1922, can set off a wave of interest in Egypt, for the most part it is international economic competition, armed conflicts, big countries generally, places where we have sentimental attachments, or the exotic that attract attention and interest. Considerable and continuing interest in Japan and things Japanese is linked to a perceived economic threat. World trouble spots like the Middle East or Central America pose a national security threat and are thus of interest. In certain communities links with the "old country," whether "Hispanic" Texas or California, "Cuban" Florida, "Scandinavian" Minnesota, "Italian" New York, or "Irish" Boston foster fuller international images.

Because governmental foreign policy is a large factor in our preoccupations, clues about where American interests might be heightened can be found in formal statements from our foreign ministry, the U.S. State Department. Speaking in April 1989 to the American Society of Newspaper Editors, Secretary of State James Baker sketched out foreign policy priorities for the United States. At the top of his list: the Soviet Union and China. Further down he mentioned the European Alliance, the Middle East, Central America and the Third World. Prior to the break-up of the Soviet Union, a useful research project would have been to track media attention to these areas and regions as the Bush administration's foreign policy evolved.

I would argue that the image of the Soviet Union in the United States is best seen through the prism of media attention (across the several functional areas) to matters deemed either important or interesting. If I were fashioning a research agenda, I would urge students to consider tracking images through rigorous analysis of some of the following areas and topics:

Superpower competition. This includes national security coverage as well as economic considerations. At least since Lincoln Steffens' visit to Russia shortly after the October 1917 revolution, when he declared, "I have seen the future and it works," attention has often been riveted on matters of competition. Nearly a half century later Nikita Khrushchev threatened to "bury" us economically. Closely linked to the general idea of national security and resultant "red scares" has been a general capitalism versus communism emphasis in our view of the rest of the world. Finally, what could have been a better metaphor for security, comparative ideologies, and national achievement than the space race, which began in the 1950s and continues in a somewhat more cooperative vein today?

Soviet leaders. Americans have had particular images of Lenin, Stalin, the one-time team of Bulganin and Khrushchev, then Khrushchev himself, Brezhnev and his short-lived successors, and, finally, Gorbachev. The image of each of these leaders has been a personification of what we thought of the country at a given time. Most Soviet leaders have been seen as threatening and less than warm and responsive individuals. For a time during World War II, when the United States and the Soviet Union were allies, Joseph Stalin was affectionately called "Uncle Joe" by Franklin D. Roosevelt, but this quickly changed after the war and as the Cold War accelerated. During this period there was an issue of *Time* that featured "Our Soviet Ally" as the cover story. The general theme was that Soviets are "just like Americans" (both had overthrown monarchies, were informal and hardwork-ing, governed by honest people, etc.). Although there have been fleetingly positive images of some Soviet leaders, it is my impres-sion that their overall portrayal in the United States has been quite negative until Mikhail Gorbachev, who is seen as a bold reformer with a Western style. So popular has Gorbachev become in U.S. media, especially after the Washington summit of December 1987, that a *New York Times* editorial in 1989 declared that if an alien arrived on the planet and asked to be taken to "your leader" in most parts of the world, the Soviet president would qualify as the most visible and exciting leader in the world today.

Soviet history. Soviets may be surprised to learn that U.S. media have often been attentive to Russian history. True, we have over-ro-manticized the Russian royal family in movies, television plays, and books, but we have carried with us images of early Russian history, great figures from the royal court and statecraft, as well as our own peculiar relations with the Soviet Union. In some instances the preoccupation with the Russian monarchy might be one way of contrasting the pre-Soviet period with what came after. Often the depictions of court life are gay and colorful, while portrayals of the period after the revolution are grim and foreboding. In fact, Amer-ican portrayals of both pre- and postrevolutionary Russians are caricatures that do little to enhance our understanding of life there. For example, our purchase of Alaska, the role of the Russians in America, including California's Fort Ross, and much more has found its way into folklore and legend. Most of this treatment is quite positive, even romantic. Media attention to the Soviet Union was occasionally linked to the passage of espionage legislation in 1917 and 1918, as well as periods of deportations and Red Scares, especially between 1917 and 1920 and 1948 to 1957.

Foreign policy conflicts. Foreign policy matters have long domi-nated our view of the Soviet Union. This goes back to conflicts with the Japanese at the turn of the century, through two world wars and, more recently, in such places as Cuba, Afghanistan, Angola, and the Middle East. Here questions are always raised about motivations: We assume that the Soviets are up to "no good," meaning activity not in the best interests of the United States, and generally this gets bad press.

Soviet science and culture. Early on, American media portrayed Soviet scientists as unimaginative copycats, stealing U.S. secrets, especially the atom bomb, although the passing of secrets was less in the realm of science than espionage. More recently there has been admiration for Soviet achievement in space sciences and other fields. Soviet scientists, of course, also became well-known in the United States because of dissident activity. On the cultural front, Soviet ballet, chess, and other artistic and cultural achievements are much admired in the United States. From the Russian literary giants such as Pushkin, Chekhov, and Dostoyevsky to composers like Tchaikovsky and Prokofiev and dancers like Nureyev and Baryshnikov, this aspect of Soviet life has generally been warmly and enthusiastically portrayed in the United States through the several media, especially television.

Civil liberties. For several decades the concept of freedom—meaning individual autonomy from the state, or the lack of it—in the Soviet Union has dominated many American images of the Soviet Union. From recent waves of immigration to Israel and the United States by Soviet Jews to the defections of dancers and KGB agents to the public protestations of the refuseniks, we have been bombarded by vivid images of people involved in a public dialogue over the meaning of freedom. More recently we have watched with fascination as that dialogue has heated up and gone public in the Soviet Union and elsewhere in the Eastern Bloc. This is of fascination and concern to many Americans, and the media pick up the beat and theme.

Sports. Soviet sports has also lingered long as an image in U.S. media. At one time the dominant image of Soviet athletes was of hefty weight lifters and professional wrestlers. More recently, and especially since the beginning of televised Olympic coverage, a much fuller picture of Soviet sports has emerged. Runners, swimmers, gymnasts, basketball players, and others have emerged. Russian and other Soviet republic athletes are increasingly seen as physically talented and attractive. The brute image remains, though: Soviets athletes are often seen as "cheaters," the "ones to beat," the "bad guys." There has also been considerable attention given to "biased" Soviet judges at the Olympics. Sports coverage of Soviets is wildly variable.

Soviet women. Soviet women have also held a fascination for U.S. media, mainly because of the range of roles they play in Soviet society. Images of female doctors, truck drivers, scientists, cosmonauts, spies, and other roles often dominated by males in the United States have intrigued American media consumers. Soviet women have enjoyed diverse images in U.S. media, from petite and elegant ballet dancers to essentially masculine (and ugly) sports competitors, engineers, and scientists. Americans have been perplexed by these images and often wonder about their accuracy and representativeness.

Peaks and valleys. U.S.-Soviet friendship has had its ups (1933-1939; 1941-1946; 1972-1978; 1986-present) and downs (every other year since 1917, the worst being 1917-1920; 1939-1940—USSR and Nazi Germany were allies; 1947-1957—the height of the Cold War; 1960-1962—Cuban crisis, Berlin Wall; 1968—Czech Invasion; 1979-1985—Afghanistan, Poland invasions), if fleeting images in U.S. media are any indication. From the days of John Reed, whose *Seven Days That Shook the World* was a best seller in its day and later inspired Warren Beatty's epic movie *Reds,* to the touching story of the 13-year-old American school girl Samantha Smith, Soviet-U.S. exchanges, from high school students to sports teams and dance companies, have been an important ingredient in any images we have of each other.

Unfortunately, the corpus of scholarship that tracks and traces images of our two countries in our respective media systems is quite limited. Some useful books and articles do exist and they add intellectual rigor to any discussion or debate of this subject. But the paucity of research suggests that much more is needed before any informed discussion of the image of the Soviet Union in the United States can be discussed seriously.

The work fostered by the Moscow State University conference is an important start, as is the writing of distinguished American contributors like George Gerbner (images of the Soviet Union in television entertainment programs), Ellen Mickiewicz (television programming) and Daniel Hallin (comparative coverage of summits). In the last two years there have been several doctoral dissertations and master's theses in the United States that take up these themes. Similarly, the work of the Center for War, Peace and the News Media at New York University has stimulated both student and faculty studies of news coverage. At three American universities that I know of—Columbia, Emory, and Michigan State—observers are tracking and studying Soviet television in joint ventures that bring specialists on Soviet affairs together with media scholars. Much of this work involves using such tools as content analysis, historical analysis, legal and regulatory study, and economic analysis. What will emerge, I believe, is a more cogent portrait of how the great superpowers see each other and themselves.

There is less attention to what this taking stock really tells us. Do these images reflect or help shape reality? Are they accurate and truthful portrayals, or misleading ones? And by whose standards? Do the mechanisms that manufacture news and create entertainment programs so deviate from the norm in the two societies that they obfuscate and obscure? More importantly, do they shape individual and institutional agendas? Do they influence thought and shape opinion? Do they, can they, influence behavior, both on a person-to-person level as well as between and among social institutions in the two societies, as well as their governments?

All these are questions that beg answers. We do not yet have an accepted, comprehensive theory of communication and media effects that provides easy or discrete answers. What we do have is an informed body of literature and experience that offers clues. Media research has moved through several cycles since it evolved as a serious intellectual pursuit earlier in this century.

As scholars have indicated elsewhere, there was initially a rather simplistic view that media were all-powerful and could have profound and controlling effects on people and culture. Then there was a long period of serious reconsideration. Study after study failed to generate evidence to prove the power of the press's ability to change behavior or even change attitudes and opinions. Later scholars focused attention on cognitive effects, guided by Bernard Cohen's suggestion that the media do not tell people what to think but what to think about. These developments in the social sciences, which offer cautious approval for the idea that the media do have powerful effects, have been augmented by humanist scholars—historians, economists, and critical theorists who believe media under certain conditions to be quite powerful. This growing literature has not been applied to the Soviet-American image situation (so far), but this ought to happen if the consequences of images are to be understood and appreciated.

What is the image of the Soviet Union in the United States? It is multifaceted and varies widely depending on what medium and what media function are being explored. The Soviet Union of the news columns and the editorial page is not the Soviet Union of the comic strips, sports pages, or television sitcoms. The Soviet Union in opinion magazines is not the Soviet Union portrayed in commercial advertising. And so it goes. Essentially, though, our understanding of the image of the Soviet Union in our media is quite primitive (as is our understanding of other nations' images) and will benefit by the current wave of interest, which is sure to bring both substantive and methodological strength to an important research venture.

9. Behind the News From Moscow[†]

Words like *remarkable* and *extraordinary* do not begin to describe the substance of news and information that began to flow from the Soviet Union to the West in the late 1980s and early 1990s.

In the years since Mikhail Gorbachev came to power and unveiled his twin policies of *glasnost* and *perestroika,* evidence of compelling change has been a daily occurrence. As consumers of news we have learned to expect the unexpected, and Soviet society seems poised for a pendulum shift. For the first time since the Cold War began, news travels with a measure of freedom; stories by Western and Soviet journalists capture the contours of a society experiencing unparalleled reexamination, redefinition, and reform.

In the midst of such fascinating information, it is easy to overlook the equally compelling changes occurring in the Soviet media system and in Soviet information policies governing Western reporters. If news is defined as the published content of the media, then the

---

† This chapter is based on two *Communiqué* columns, "Behind the News From Moscow," September 1989 and "Rumors and Gossip in the USSR," May 1990 (monthly newsletter of FFMSC).

nature and dimensions of what constitutes news in the Soviet republics are changing radically.

So is the role of the Soviet journalists, whose freedom to report and write about governmental policies, ethnic disputes, the environment, the military, and other vital topics has increased considerably. People speak about investigative reporting, more ambitious attempts to get information from reluctant governmental sources, and much more.

To be sure, the Soviet media are still an integral part of the state, and journalists do not present themselves as an independent force, let alone a fourth estate. But this caveat notwithstanding there is remarkable change in Soviet media: Gosteleradio, the state broadcasting system, now telecasts the Supreme Soviet much as C-SPAN covers Capitol Hill; and progressive papers have become vessels for discussion and debate.

Soviet media scholars are watching these changes closely, asking questions about what structures will work best in the future for this complex and far-flung collection of print and electronic voices. Indeed for them—and for us—the highly visible consequences of Glasnost are perhaps less compelling than the debate over whether the economic incentives introduced by *perestroika* might also apply to Soviet media, which are not yet "industries" in the Western sense, but which are considering democratic models and entrepreneurial approaches to make them more globally competitive.

U.S. media scholars, a few with expertise about the Soviet Union, have joined the international community of scholars who, with different approaches, ideologies, and concerns, are making important comparisons between Soviet and Western media and between and among papers and programs as disparate as *Pravda* and the *New York Times, Izvestia* and the *Washington Post*, "Vremya" and ABC's "World News Tonight." The several recent U.S.-Soviet summits have been analyzed carefully, as have the images of the two countries in entertainment programming. A research agenda, one that will help the two countries better understand each other, is just beginning to take shape.

This important research is emerging at the same time that our concepts about the impact and influence of the media on individuals, institutions and society are undergoing significant change. What a time to engage in comparative studies of U.S. and Soviet media— on issues such as their role vis-à-vis government, their political economy, reporting styles and standards, and the education of journalists.

Rumors and Gossip in the Soviet Union

The continuing transformation of the news media in the Soviet Union still surprises observers as old taboos give way to a livelier, more candid form of journalism. Typically this is portrayed in the West as a good thing, the freeing up of media beset with censorship both official and self-imposed.

On a visit to Moscow I witnessed yet another innovation in Soviet journalism—the emergence of gossip, of speculative reports based on rumor rather than official pronouncement. An issue of the progressive and highly critical *Moscow News* carried an item with the headline "Moscovites Talking—Rumors and Izvestia" over a story that declared: "Life without rumors is dull, but life without 'izvestia' (news) or reliable information is dangerous."

Then, incredibly, the article—signed "V.T."—explained how Moscow was rife with rumors about who would be the new editor of *Izvestia*, the official organ of the Soviet parliament and "the paper of Glasnost." The editor's seat had opened up when Ivan Laptev became chairman of one of the chambers of parliament, which gave rise in the article to the speculation about who would be his successor.

In that I was part of a delegation whose appointment with Mr. Laptev had been canceled, the article was of considerable interest. As I read on I saw what Soviet readers rarely see—names of possible successors and even the bold suggestions that maybe the staff should elect the editor.

As with gossip and speculation elsewhere in the world, the *Moscow News* report was incomplete. It failed to report a matter of fact—that members of *Izvestia's* staff had petitioned Gorbachev to listen to their recommendations for the editorship, another act that is rare if not unprecedented for journalists in the Soviet Union. And very much like stories in the West, the factual case was more interesting than the rumors, which one analyst told me were not well informed at all.

Still, the phenomenon of the rumors was an important development in the transformation of Soviet journalism. Did the *Moscow News* article represent a transposition of bad habits from the West, in which our gossip machine seems to have gone wild, or did it mark a natural progression in freedom of expression?

As we see change in the Soviet press—incremental at first but increasingly more brisk—we are witnessing a major change in the definition of news. Some of that change leans toward a Western style of journalism, some simply reflects a written version of what was always on people's tongues in private conversation. But the net result is a creative, new chorus of journalistic voices from diverse publications that range from party and governmental organs to those of the army, youth groups, and other social interests.

It is clear to Western observers that the changes in old restrictions in the Soviet Union—which appear at this writing to be quite fragile—will bring performances both exemplary and exploitative. If Western media critics could have their way and help the Soviets and East Europeans transform their media systems, they would likely urge excellence and probably not welcome gossip columnists, rumor mongers and sloppy and incomplete reportage. But then, too, the people who are the ultimate consumers of media want to be informed, entertained, persuaded, consoled—perhaps even courted and cajoled.

The changes we witness elsewhere in the world provide a mirror for our own media as we consider anew their functions, performance and ability to stimulate our interests, thoughts and passions.

Earlier in this century while on a visit to the Soviet Union, Lincoln Steffens declared that he had seen the future and it works; today observers in the Soviet Union can claim to have seen sweeping change amid great impediments to change. The outcome of Glasnost and Perestroika may be hugely influenced by communication both within the Soviet Union and outside, but especially between us and them, the old combatants in the Cold War.

10. Journalistic Aid to Eastern Europe[†]

Throughout the Cold War the media of the Soviet Union and other Warsaw Pact states were strident defenders of their system, a part and parcel of the state. In the aftermath of upheaval in Eastern Europe and change in the Soviet Union, some of the Communist world's new media leaders say the "party line" press, an instrument

---

† This chapter is based on two *Communiqué* columns, "Journalistic Aid to Eastern Europe," February 1990 and "Reconsidering Eastern Bloc Media," December 1989 (monthly newsletter of FFMSC).

of government policy and propaganda, must change. Whether that change will be a media version of "socialism with a human face," in Alexander Dubcek's phrase, or some new formulation is not yet clear.

What is clear is that change has come with dramatic bursts. It is too soon to tell just what the long-term implications of Glasnost and Perestroika are for the Soviet and Eastern European media, but it is evident that the role of the press is being redefined, that the news and information reaching people are fundamentally different, and that the role of those engaged in journalism is also shifting. Some leaders in Eastern Europe readily admit they need to seriously reconsider the purposes of public communication, perhaps taking a lesson or two from the West, especially from the United States.

Regardless of ideology, there is much to be said for Jeremy Tunstall's assertion that "the media are American." Much of modern mass media was invented in the United States, developed and nurtured by our economic, legal, and political system.

Without presumptuously trying to impose our media system on others, we could take important strides by sharing knowledge and technical information with those interested in it. International media organizations in the West like the International Press Institute and the International Institute of Communications could open discussions with and offer assistance to their Eastern counterparts. Industry groups like the American Newspaper Publishers Association, the American Society of Newspaper Editors, the National Association of Broadcasters and the Radio and Television News Directors Association could do likewise. Journalism and communication schools also have much to offer and to learn from their counterparts in Eastern Europe. Perhaps, too, there is a role for UNESCO in establishing a formal structure for more interaction between media people and media systems formerly so much at odds that they had little to discuss.

The discussion of the role and function of the press, whether fostering conflict or cooperation between different groups, has of course long been a topic of discussion in the United States. Our own debates on a range of issues demonstrate that we have not yet discovered a single purpose or formula for news and information. Importantly, however, we operate a press system that is separate from government without being essentially hostile to it.

We have now an unprecedented opportunity to offer support of a psychological, professional, and technical nature to the transforming media systems of Eastern Europe. If we are, in fact, seeing the beginning of the end of the Cold War, the most vital indicator of change will be in the public communication system that emerges, whether incrementally or with a pendulum swing. Whether in the end the Soviet-Eastern bloc media come to resemble their Western counterparts or develop some other quasi-governmental press systems is anyone's guess, but to the extent that all communications have common elements and share some values, there can be no better time to extend our friendship and offers of a supportive forum for interaction.

Reconsidering Eastern European Media

For years we have debated the role of the media in the Soviet Union and Eastern Europe, comparing it with the media's role in our system and asking whether their messages have had the same degree of believability and credibility that ours have.

Although no definitive research provides ready answers, there is also no reason to believe that the people on the other side of what was the Cold War are any less dependent on their media for understanding society and the world than we are. They may bring degrees of skepticism or belief to the news they receive but it is clear that they read and consume it in large numbers.

Now the media of the Soviet Union and Eastern Europe seem to be redefining, even reinventing themselves. In the midst of this change some voices in the Warsaw Pact nations are looking to the West for ideas and even for aid. And many in the West are responding, some eager to implant Western-style freedom in heretofore unreceptive places, others seeking joint ventures in the emerging communications industry in Eastern Europe, and still others promoting values of professionalism and training.

While remembering that media people in these strife-torn countries will want to fashion their own systems, we can with friendship offer to interpret the virtues (and vices) of our system to those in previously closed societies who are interested in knowing what we do and how we do it.

In several respects, we in the West can join in a productive dialogue if we consider both the most pervasive and the most practical aspects of our communication system as it relates to other countries.

It will not be enough to offer journalistic aid to Eastern European colleagues if we do not also consider some or all of the following:

- What structural and legal/constitutional guarantees are necessary to assure free expression and a free press in a given country?
- What are the economic conditions that make a modern system of communication (and media industries) work effectively and efficiently?
- What, if any, universal values are essential to a modern press and communication system?
- What kinds of technical knowledge and assistance can help fledgling media survive and prosper in a transitional society?
- What kinds of education and training for journalists, broadcasters, media managers, and other personnel are needed in an evolving communication system?
- What lessons are there for the West in comparative analysis and evaluation of new media enterprises in the socialist world?

We need to approach our new media relations with these countries and societies carefully and with respect. Whatever lasting changes occur may have a great deal to do with our actions and activities in the coming months and years.

We may also learn something about ourselves that will be enormously beneficial in the process. If we are wise enough to look at the waning of the Cold War not in terms of winners and losers but with a spirit of human cooperation, we may avoid unnecessarily patronizing attitudes that will engender new conflicts and misunderstandings. Though we may not agree on every political nuance of these emerging media systems, there are other areas, such as the environment, in which the notion of one world communicating freely would have immediate value.

Thus I believe that while having something very substantial to offer people fashioning new media systems in countries such as Poland, Czechoslovakia, and the Soviet Union, we also have something to learn about one another in the process. What happens in the Warsaw Pact press will inevitably have some impact on our own media system. We just might engage in a cultural conversation with a payoff for people everywhere, especially if the result is a more honest and credible global media system.

11. The Search for Freedom of the Press[†]

This essay describes a variety of impressions from a fact finding trip I took on behalf of the Gannett Foundation to Central and Eastern Europe in the summer of 1990. The foundation, which is greatly concerned with freedom of the press, was naturally interested in a first-hand report on the developments in that region of the world where so much happened in 1989-1990; years in which governments fell and new leadership emerged—devoted, they said, to freedom of all kinds, especially freedom of the press.

We have read about these developments in newspapers and magazines, and personally witnessed them on our television screens as the Berlin Wall crumbled and as a magnificent "velvet revolution" swept across other countries of the region. And although we may know of the role of the press and television both there and here in that process, we rarely think about these developments in a communications context.

To do so, let me touch on just a few of the images of our recent visit. In an office at Charles University in Prague, Czechoslovakia, I met an educator who more than 20 years ago was a young editor at the time of the Prague Spring. He was banished from journalism and forced to work as a window washer for 20 years. He returned and began to build a new journalism school dedicated to press freedom rather than propaganda values.

Another person, an editor and critic in Warsaw, Poland, laid out on the floor of his apartment for us issues of his magazine that had been published during the underground period. Occasionally there were missing issues, marking the times he spent in jail, sometimes being tortured. And there is yet another image fresh in my mind of a young broadcast station manager in Belgrade, Yugoslavia, who was recruited for his job by his 20-year-old colleagues who had only recently taken over the station. He was elected to his position in 1990

[†] This chapter is based on a September 20, 1990 speech "The Search for Freedom of the Press in the United States and Eastern Europe," Brigham Young University, Provo, Utah, and the *Communiqué* column of July/August 1990, "Can There Be an Ideal Press Law?" (monthly newsletter of FFMSC).

and said he would have to stand for reelection in six months. I also think of young Americans in most of the capitals we visited. These people have come to what they regard as one of the most exciting places on the globe today to watch new societies develop and to assist in the process if they can. They have come to learn and to help, and, believe me, the opportunities open to them in this fast-paced and fragile region are unlike any others that a typical internship would afford. It may be a long time before we know and understand all the facets of just how the velvet revolution of 1989 occurred in Central and Eastern Europe—who was responsible and who played what role—but it is clear to most observers that the *samizdat* (underground) press played a very large role.

An incipient free *samizdat* press hid for many years. On occasion its editors and reporters were caught, sent to prison, even tortured. Today that underground press, or in some cases its successor papers and magazines, is alive and well in the countries I visited, namely Czechoslovakia, Hungary, Poland, and Yugoslavia.

In these four countries there is evidence of new voices everywhere—on the newsstands, in the kiosks, being hawked by people on the streets. People line up in Prague or in Budapest and in many smaller cities awaiting news and excitement contained in the papers and sheets being published that day. It is a city with every manner of free expression—some of it noble and serious, some of it outrageous and sensational. Pornography, in particular, has become plentiful. Those who look closely at the media in these countries see profound and significant changes in radio and on television. For example, electronic media, once run by the Communist government with strong Soviet influence, now have new masters. They are still run by governments, but governments that are, to date, democratic and devoted to freedom.

One also sees hundreds of weekly papers and magazines, as well as scores of dailies, that have emerged to cover the news and express opinions about the need for change. There, too, where the literacy rate is about 92% to 98%—compared with our paltry 85% rate in the United States—book publishing is also flourishing. For more than 40 years, the structure was the message in these countries. Government not only controlled the media but also carefully crafted bureaucracies that split apart the various aspects of the media, putting each under a different control mechanism. For example, a newspaper was simply an editorial office. In order to get its material printed, the staff had to beg permission from a government printing office. And then, sometime later, they would make a similar case to a government distribution office. Of course, those elements were all orchestrated by a central government, but by no means was the resulting process efficient or effective for the newspaper. As we look at this region today and recognize the very real differences between and among these quite distinctive countries, we can detect several common threads. By the end of 1990, each country was at work on new press laws to incorporate into their new constitutions and legal systems. They are actually defining freedom of the press and trying to determine what, if any, exceptions should be made. Some new laws resemble our own First Amendment while others are more complex and cumbersome.

Concurrent with the writing of new media laws, the people in the four countries I visited were also fashioning a new market economy to replace the former command or centralized economy of the Soviet-style government. This is a transitional process; much of the old state enterprise still exists, especially the state printing and newspaper distribution services. Gradually, however, advertising has come into the media and there is other evidence of a free market economy. One feature of these changes is the introduction of foreign investment, as international media companies and other entrepreneurs buy into the press of the region.

Even the system of education and journalism training in Eastern Europe is undergoing considerable reform. Old journalism instructors in universities with a Marxist-Leninist orientation are being replaced by faculties similar to those in the West. Journalism associations, long responsible for professional training and development, are also reorganizing themselves. Some of these changes are quite wrenching—people are displaced as old faculties and journalist associations seek new credibility. This is a quite unsettled area, and one that could benefit from Western training aids. In addition to these insider matters, there are also many public considerations about the press in these countries. Journalists and others are trying to determine what kind of press and what style of journalism best suit the public, and which approach will be accepted by a public that is making a free choice for the first time.

As we look at these momentous and sweeping changes in a region that is arguably the most exciting in the world for communicators, these changes demand that we reflect on our own media. After all, those of us involved in aid efforts of various kinds are not simply urging people in other countries to adopt our system, which probably would not fit their needs, but instead to develop their own unique system and approach.

Can There Be an Ideal Press Law?

In an era of new beginnings and radical change in several countries on the globe, increasingly there is talk of the ideal press law, the ultimate compact among people, government, and media.

In Eastern Europe such explorations are under way. At this writing in Russia, the Supreme Soviet was formulating a new press law, and similarly in China a press law research center is moving thoughtfully toward recommendations that will assure freedom of expression. A delegation from the Chinese center came to visit us in June of 1990, asking questions about the nature and status of our own system of freedom of expression.

Explaining our constitutional scheme for press freedom to foreign visitors looking for the legal equivalent of zero-based budgeting is not an easy task. After all, we have a system that is at once simple and complex. Nothing could be simpler and more unequivocal than the First Amendment's command to "make no law . . . abridging freedom of speech, or of the press," but even that spare language is, arguably, rich with ambiguity. That simple expression, which Justice Hugo Black used to say "means just what it says it does," lives alongside a massive array of federal and state statutes, court decisions, and legal interpretations that add up to a very complex and often confusing communication law.

We generally agree on such principles as forbidding the prior restraint of communication, but even that linchpin concept is challenged at times by government secrecy and combative adversaries in the private sector who would control information and restrict public access. Although we know that our system was established to allow for the free flow of information and the dissemination of opinions, we also know that such seemingly uncontroversial ideas often come into conflict with defamation, obscenity, privacy, and proprietary information.

When we look closely at our constitutional scheme and the many efforts to clarify its meaning, it is clear that we have not even determined whether freedom of the press is an affirmative right that belongs to all citizens—that is, the listeners—or only an institutional right that belongs to those who own and operate newspapers, television stations, and media companies.

We speak of the rights of a free press but avoid the corollary notion of duties, arguing that the Constitution says nothing about obligations or responsibilities. Indeed that is the reason we do not license journalists or impose legally binding press codes or ethical rules. Theoretically, at least, we defend the most elegant and responsible expression as well as the most scurrilous. All are entitled to free expression, though they may be held accountable in court after the fact if it is determined that one person's press freedom has intruded on the rights of others.

We tell our visitors looking curiously at the U.S. press system about the great lessons of cases like *Near v. Minnesota* or *New York Times v. Sullivan* and at the same time admit instances in which both have been challenged or ignored.

We explain the Fourth Estate, the notion of the press as a representative of the people but also say this is more a metaphor than a legal reality.

Still, to the extent that our system works at all it must thank public confidence in government and assumptions about freedom in the abstract against which day-to-day disputes can be measured. We confess to our visitors our occasional discomfort with a system that posits absolute freedom in the Bill of Rights but that also allows for multimillion dollar libel suits that clearly chill expression.

It is, we admit, an imperfect system, but one that has some grand principles and some general acceptance on a playing field that, though not always level, at least affords a chance for public combat in fashioning and defining freedom.

We tell our Eastern European, Soviet, and Chinese colleagues to keep it simple, to get clearly defined rights in place, but know in the end that even under the best of circumstances they, like us, will discover that liberty of expression is a dynamic bargaining game subject to all kinds of human error.

Still, as we look at the evolving press laws in these countries, we ought to ask questions about our own press freedom, which, though guaranteed by the First Amendment, is administered with great complexity by volumes of press laws and media regulations that are anything but simple.

We also recognize the paradox of our system, which on the one hand promotes a free enterprise press but sometimes requires government intervention to keep the press free and protect the public. On such issues as fraudulent advertising, libel, pornography, and others, intervention has long been accepted in a society that generally opposes government involvement in the media.

And what about our own market economy? Is it a great model for others? Ours may be the most successful commercial media system in the world, but it has flaws. As a society we are quite undecided about what is the best pattern of media ownership and just how media revenues should be raised. This is a matter of continuous debate.

Although we eschew government involvement per se in much of our media, we also have joint-operating agreements that are actually government-sanctioned arrangements by which the press in particular areas is made exempt from antitrust laws. Looking at our own system of journalism education may make us wonder whether our model is appropriate for others, or even ourselves, under all conditions. True, we have what most of us believe is the best system of communication education in the world, but at the same time it has detractors, many of them in the media, who would themselves create some other kind of system.

My point here is that we may have as much to learn from Eastern Europe as we have to gain. It will, like learning a foreign language, make us more conscious of our own *lingua franca* in media. It will help us understand, critique, and appreciate our own system more as we look carefully at the ones arising in these new societies.

Amidst this intoxicating atmosphere of freedom of expression, there is, of course, a downside that will get worse as economic pressures mount. There will no doubt be considerable unemployment in once fully employed societies, and some of that unemployment will occur in the media.

In this brief essay, I have tried to convey a glimpse of the images of a media system in its infancy. It is a system growing up in a part of the world that may just be the most exciting place on earth to watch in the 1990s.

12. Television and the Bamboo Curtain†

At no time has the global impact of television been more evident than during the 1989 student demonstration and devastation in Tiananmen Square. In a country where government once had all-

---

† *Communiqué* column, June 1989 (monthly newsletter of FFMSC).

powerful control over the ebb and flow of news and information, a new force has taken hold.

Aided by technology—including communication satellites and fax machines—communication from China is no longer constrained by national boundaries or even government edicts. Although for a time U.S. and other television networks had their transmissions halted, this short-lived effort to stop the flow of information failed precisely because it focused attention on Chinese government efforts to quell dissent and prevent outsiders from seeing the turmoil in their society.

What a distance we have traveled from the 1970s, when we still relied on interpretations of wall posters in Hong Kong to guess what was happening in China.

Television coverage of the sit-ins and demonstrations in Beijing's Tiananmen Square was also aided by increasing demands for more freedom within the Chinese media. Newspapers like the *People's Daily*, the Xinhau official news agency, central television and radio, along with media-savvy student activists carrying placards with legends in English, French, and simplified Chinese characters, all aimed at overseas audiences. In a real sense the students in the square were excellent spin doctors—media consultants without portfolios who nonetheless knew how to attract attention and win favorable news coverage abroad.

Although the Chinese people had little or no opportunity to see the coverage of the demonstrations that American audiences watched, it was clear that news of its international impact was trickling down; public announcements about martial law and the abrupt and uncertain nature of Chinese news coverage of events indicated as much.

It is much too soon to assess just what if any permanent impact this unprecedented media coverage will have on international diplomacy, the Chinese central power structure, or world opinion. It was clear that try though they might the Chinese officials could not control the embarrassing spectacle in Tiananmen Square in the short run, not even with the tools of martial law. The news reached people around the globe, who responded with demonstrations of support. Official communiqués from usually cautious governments hedged their bets on which faction they thought would win out.

A revolution, if this was one, is both a thrilling and a terrible event to cover. With predictable parochialism, U.S. media coverage portrayed the Chinese crisis as a fairly simple suit for freedom by the students and their supporters, mostly in Beijing, at times comparing it enthusiastically to the American and French revolutions. We saw the Chinese through American eyes, wherein American symbols and conventions were invoked to make the scene from the square more understandable to American audiences.

The American networks, especially CNN and CBS, were hailed by many critics for their stunning on-the-scene portrayals, but other news outlets demonstrated that they too could do multifaceted coverage, mixing the reports of resident correspondents with the insights of experts and specialists back home.

If there was a disturbing aspect of the American coverage it was the understandably overplayed scene from the square to the exclusion of activities elsewhere in China, where there were fewer correspondents and other news resources.

At no time was there comprehensive treatment of the scope and intensity of the student fury, the extent of its support, and the likely consequence for Chinese communication policy and public opinion. We also have no idea what the Chinese people knew and when they knew it. In a country where centralized state broadcasting is still the rule, it is impossible to predict just how people got the news and how they responded to it.

Moreover the paucity of good scholarship on international communication and the role of the media in political transitions was not much help in informing the coverage or analysis of the Chinese upheaval. Neither, of course, was the lack of cultural literacy of Americans toward Chinese language, culture, government, and public life.

Although the theme "love of freedom" was evident throughout the coverage, one could not help wondering to what extent our media were being co-opted and manipulated by the friendly faces in the Beijing crowd. Knowing so little, we relied on television news to make sense out of a highly charged and complex affair where our own impressions helped shape our views. Yet for all of television's great power, it gave us only a marginal understanding of a still mysterious society.

PART III

On Educating Communicators

13. Educating the University[†]

Communications studies in the American university are beset by a curious paradox: there is hardly an intelligent person alive who does not readily agree that communications is central to human enterprise and existence, but few are aware that there is a field devoted to communications research. Many might even agree that the role of the media is becoming even more important as events in China and Eastern Europe so clearly demonstrated in the late 1980s. The revolutions of 1989 and 1990 were profoundly influenced by communications and communications systems.

In Central and Eastern Europe, communication was not only a vehicle for the revolution (and the supplier of many of its leaders) but also an object of revolution. Remember that the media were the central nervous system of the old Communist order that was largely replaced during the several revolutions—some of them velvet, and others with harder edges. As we look at the recent leadership of countries like Czechoslovakia and Poland, for example, we see presidents, prime ministers, foreign ministers, and others who have come from the media to their new posts. Well beyond the case of Eastern Europe, none would seriously argue that it is possible to understand electoral politics, consumer behavior, or any of the many facets of public life without understanding the role of communication media and the process of communication itself. Is there a subject, a field, a phenomenon, where communication does not play a leading role? The answer, I think, is evident in this inquiry, which reifies our dependence on communication.

Still, there seem to be few links between general public understanding of the role and impact of communication and its role in the American university. To the extent that communication is recognized as a field of study, or even a discipline, it exists in a somewhat sleepy,

† Speech delivered at a colloquium of the Department of Communication at the University of Michigan, "Educating the University About Communications: An Agenda for Students, Society, and the 'The Usual Suspects,' " October 4, 1990.

stable state, hardly on the cutting edge of what most universities regard as their most important endeavors. Indeed, I can only think of two or three university presidents in the United States who publicly acknowledge that communications study is high on their personal agendas.

There are two basic reasons for this: a serious identity and credibility problem. This was once pointed out to me in a conversation with the long-time head of research at McGraw-Hill, Dr. David Forsyth, who later became head of the department of communications at Brigham Young University in Provo, Utah. Dr. Forsyth said that when he told colleagues in the media industries that he was going to head a communications department, they asked him what that was. But when he mentioned the various components—journalism, broadcasting, communication research, they instantly understood.

This inspired him to do a study asking people in universities, the media industries, and other institutions what "communications" in the university context meant to them. He also looked broadly at what various "communication" departments in the United States call themselves and found a wide nomenclature.

In further conversations with university colleagues, he was told that a communications department is presumptuous because it claims so much of the territory covered by psychologists, sociologists, political scientists, philosophers, and many others. Those Dr. Forsyth spoke to thought that in the face of presumptuous claims of competence (and territory), that communications departments deliver too little. In what is often an administrative convenience, journalism and speech-communication departments come under an umbrella called *communication* even though the term does not communicate clear information to university colleagues, let alone the media industries or the general public.

I have encountered this identity problem on a number of occasions over the years. One vivid memory I have was at the University of Oregon, where a proposal to merge two well-established university departments under the name *communication* brought protests from mathematicians, sociologists, and speech professors, who thought that communication was clearly their domain.

Beyond the issue of identity, there is within the university and the professional community a continuing problem of credibility. In Gertrude Stein's phrase, our colleagues often ask whether "there is any there there?" The problem is not that there is too little territory to traverse, but that there is too much. We claim at times to have a mastery of interpersonal and group communications, of mass communication and media studies, of journalism, advertising, public relations, and visual communication. We merge and blend substantive areas of scholarship, such as the history, economics, and sociology of our field, with professional practice. We acknowledge in broad contours two ways of knowing: that derived from professional experience; and that derived from systematic study, from scholarship. Yet, within each of these categories is vast diversity.

For example, when we speak with pride of the professional media credentials and the experience of our faculties we speak of high-, intermediate- and low-level experience in various media. We blend reporting with editing and management expertise. And we do not distinguish differences very often.

As for scholarly preparation and experience, we eclectically accept both social scientific and humanistic backgrounds. We recognize such tools as historiography, survey research, content analysis, legal analysis, econometrics, literary criticism, and critical studies.

Stepping back from our real world and academic embrace of communications, we might ask whether we are appropriately celebrating eclecticism, or rather are mired down in meaningless fragmentation. In short, do we know what we are talking about and is there evidence to prove it?

Although we now see few "state-of-the-field" reviews of the kind that scholars like Wilbur Schramm and Bernard Berelson used to deliver, we are benefitting today from the work of scholars who want to uncover the roots of communications research and media studies, and who in the process make us proud of our origins and the yield of our multifaceted, patchwork-quilt field. In recent years, colleagues like Everett Rogers, Jesse Delia, Ellen Wartella, James Carey, John Peters, and James Anderson, just to name a few, have begun exploring the history of communications research, opening an important self-examination about the role and quality of the work in this field.

As we reflect on these and other assessments, it is plain to me that we need to state clearly just what we are. Our dual identity and credibility problem is both clarified and confused by stating that we are what we do. Think of it when we declare, that

- We are the curriculum; that is, we are what we teach or say we teach.
- We are the yield of our research and what it says.

- We are a reflection of ourselves in our service; that is, what the outside world sees of our efforts.

Another way to focus this field is to examine communications curricula we provide for students. How coherent is that pathway as we are driven by consumerism (teaching what students want to take) while trying to defend vital subject matter (that which might not be popular or valued)?

In contrast with a traditional academic discipline like history, which knows what it is, communications educators often fall short, organizing resources and commitments on the basis of what students say they want. It has been this consumer-oriented thrust that has expanded the public relations component of communications departments, while diminishing journalism. It has favored how-to craft courses over seemingly less urgent conceptual courses. We need to ask more often whether there really is a core that all students of communication must have. Is there a settled body of knowledge, however it is delivered—whether in courses, texts, or other means— that all students must have to be educated persons in the field of communication? If there is, we do not say so very often, nor do we adequately debate and codify our field.

We have the experience of journalism education, in which the tension between craft and concept, between the market and the academy, between the ideal education and job-readiness, leads more often to confusion than to coherence and agreement. It is not, necessarily, a bad thing, but it does represent a very real challenge to organize the results of such discourse into a curriculum and a research agenda that inspires public confidence and allows for a clear identity.

I recall a visit to Rutgers University a few years ago when the fields of communication, journalism, and librarianship were being organized under a single administrative structure. Disparate elements were brought together probably more for administrative convenience than for common intellectual ground, although one could argue that all of the joined elements were concerned with the acquisition, processing, and dissemination of information. I was greatly impressed by a document issued in this department at the time of the merger of speech and journalism that rather effectively articulated underlying and unifying purposes.

In a sense, we are blessed by the ever-expanding subject matter of this field. Just a few years ago, it was possible to describe the typical university department of communications with a few buzz words describing curriculum, research, and service imperatives. Today, we have added the economics of communication; media sociology; technology studies; policy analysis, including public and private sector connections; regulatory issues; communication law; and international communication; and even such specialized arenas as environmental communications, health communications, and cultural studies.

Amid these evolving interests, it is important not to forget our principal obligations to students, the university, and to society. For students we ought to:

- Draw a conceptual map of the field and require mastery of the nature, scope, and range of communications studies, typically with specific knowledge in a single area; for undergraduates this means an "acquaintance with" the field and its meaning; for graduate students, more rigor and depth.
- Connect communications studies with the rest of the university, helping students see their complete education through a communications prism.
- And link communications studies to careers, and even lifestyles, as well as society itself. We ought to be able to help students use communications to achieve their own personal goals and objectives whether they enter the field professionally or not.

We typically try to do these things through majors, minors, cognates, and concentrations. It may also be useful to offer helpful consultation to students as they consider the communications teachings of other fields. How many know whether the view of politics and the media as presented in the field of political science squares with the best contemporary research? Or whether advertising as portrayed in economics courses connects with interpretations from media studies?

In many universities there is little consistency between other "communications teachings" and those in the communication or journalism department or school itself. I am not suggesting that one view is right and another wrong, but inconsistencies of interpretation and ways of knowing ought to be pointed out to students.

It might also be useful for communication faculty members to take this conversation beyond their offices and engage in an active dialogue with colleagues from other fields. This would also have the advantage of letting others in the university know that there is a body of knowledge in communication with something to offer. As for society, we communications scholars have an obligation:

- To foster understanding of communication phenomena for individuals and for institutions.
- To assist citizens in developing critical media consumer skills.
- To promote better use of communication in public life for problem identification and solutions.

These goals for students and for society are noble, but just how do we accomplish them? Teaching, research, and service are not enough. We must add public scholarship to the list. We need to be more effective public scholars in a fashion that links systematic knowledge to public discussion and possibly even public policy.

We might do this in several different ways. In my own experience at our center at Columbia Unversity, we accidentally got into public scholarship as the result of high-profile conferences, seminars, and publications. The work of our fellows and staff began to attract public attention and got covered on its own merits.

We see our role as that of sense-maker, explaining when we can what parties are interested in a given public issue, whether it is a cable bill before Congress or an economic trend affecting the newspaper industry. We try to sort out issues and offer analysis and context. Typically, we do not take positions, believing that there really are multiple ways of knowing, though some sources and positions are based on sounder evidence than others. We would like to think that we are impartial in these responses. From the standpoint of the Gannett Center, though the staff and I try to play a neutral role, our fellows are free to take forceful positions as long as they do not purport to speak for the institution, which is funded by tax-free dollars.

I would like to see the field of communications studies, either at individual universities or through its several professional associations, do on a much larger scale what we are doing at the Gannett Center. Although this is a rather elaborate and demanding approach, it is not such a complex effort for each faculty member to have a communication plan for his or her own work. I am often surprised at what a terrible job some of our communication faculty colleagues do in promoting their own work. Not only do they not send reprints and advance copies to fellow scholars or interested professionals but they rarely think of putting their work in the hands of media decision-makers, columnists, the trade press, or other possible sources that can extend their work through public attention.

Some people prefer to opt out of the public dialogue, but far more want to be a part of it without knowing how. Faculty members, for instance, often complain that nobody pays any attention to their work, but at the same time they do little to promote it or themselves. It is possible they do not know how, and in such cases it would be useful for our professional associations like the International Communication Association, the Association for Education in Journalism and Mass Communication, or the Speech Communication Association to help them through workshops and consultation services that will advance communications studies through public discourse.

The public has a right and a need to be exposed to media issues, especially when they are pertinent to public issues. Again, we have done this recently through the *Media Studies Journal,* which, in an issue covering the environment, engaged economists, scientists, journalists, and educators in a symposium that looked at environmental coverage.

Sometimes it is useful to bring the public into one of our well-developed "knowledge arenas," such as health communications, and show how applied research on health awareness helped combat public ignorance about AIDS in a manner that helped shape attitudes and perhaps even behavior.

There may be less interest in what might be called our "intramural" discussions, such as the rise of critical media studies, which is somewhat akin to critical legal studies. Though this trend in our field is on the rise, few scholars or administrators are willing to discuss it in public with, for example, media professionals, fearing perhaps a kind of 1990s McCarthyism. Far better that we engage in this debate on our own terms today, however, than have it discovered by unfriendly critics in the future and become the stuff of a mean and punitive battle whereby academic freedom is impaired.

There are other areas that could provide a useful public discussion, or at least one that is pertinent within the media or media studies family. Often, though, we are too busy to consider such vital communication of our own work or concerns.

My emphasis here is in promoting, publicizing, and making more effective use of our own work and ideas. There is another service we might perform. In every university community there are professors expert in a given field who are mavens for the media on that subject. We see Soviet history specialists, American politics teachers, and others speaking out as expert witnesses in the media. They are sometimes called "the usual suspects," because of their frequent appearance on television or in the public print media. It is a role I frequently play at Columbia.

But I have at least one advantage over many of my colleagues in other fields who engage in this same type of activity: I know something about how media work and why. I generally know what to expect from a reporter and how to be genuinely helpful. Of course this is also true of many faculty members in communications studies and journalism departments. What these people have is substantive knowledge and technical expertise that can be helpful to others in the university, not just in a public relations sense, but in fostering real understanding of the media and communications as well as our role as individual sources. The nature and consequences of media contact is something worthy of thought and analysis. Here we have real knowledge and experience we can offer to our colleagues in other fields, both to help them and to help our universities become more effective public communicators.

When once I suggested such assistance, I was told that people from other fields are not exactly beating down the doors for such consultation. There are obvious ways to make such connections, whether through personal contact, seminars, and other faculty development programs. Here is a chance for communications studies to take the high road, looking at "the usual suspects" as they relate to science news, politics, economics, and other fields.

Such an effort at public scholarship in this field, and public scholarship awareness and assistance for other fields, would have obvious benefits. It would make the university more relevant to society. It would enhance scholarship and individual scholars as they engage more often in public dialogue. For many in the university, it might link them to a public conversation from which they are now excluded.

As you can see, it is important to do a better job of educating the university for and about communications. We need to do a better job of bringing into focus the great communication issues of our

time. Along the way, as we consider these vital forces, we might just
help enhance the quality of the media and of the communication
work force. We might also upgrade the awareness and even the
competence of our citizens as consumers of communications. And
for our own field or discipline (take your pick), we can stake out a
territory with a clear identity and real credibility.

14. Communication Education and Its Critics[†]

Communication education has more than its share of critics. Although higher education generally and professional schools such as
business, law, and education are the subjects of reform proposals,
communication and journalism schools seem to attract even more
scrutiny than their professional school counterparts. Wondering
whether this impression was sound, I decided to look at more than
twenty articles in professional, trade, and popular magazines over
the last decade.[1] I compared these with published critiques of other
kinds of professional schools during the same period. All professional schools were criticized by voices outside major professional
constituencies. Within higher education itself, professional schools
were also found wanting, regarded as out of tune with the academic
culture, and lacking in intellectual vigor.

My review revealed that critics of other professional schools were
typically less shrill than those commenting on the communication
and journalism schools. Some critics were especially harsh, such as
those who blamed ruthless behavior on Wall Street on M.B.A. training or the existence of mercenary lawyers on legal education. Nevertheless, the other professional schools seemed to have more friends,
more cheerleading enthusiasts who wrote warmly, even sentimen-
tally, about the contributions of these educational efforts to individuals and their respective professions. Recall that legal education
even got a movie, *The Paper Chase*.

† This chapter originally appeared January 1990 as an article in the *Syracuse Scholar*,
101.

Nearly twenty-five years ago I enrolled in the master's program at the newly renamed Newhouse School of Communications at Syracuse University (the "Public" came later; even earlier it had been a school of journalism). I knew little of the academic and professional pressures facing that school and others like it. But I was struck by the way the school presented itself to new students, especially in a little booklet about the faculty, *The Log*, which took its title from a statement by President James A. Garfield: "The ideal college is a log, with the student at one end and Mark Hopkins at the other."[2]

That compact publication carried striking pictures of the Newhouse faculty and an outline of their attainments. Prospective students got an impressive list of positions the faculty had held in major media, books they had written, and organizations for which they had consulted. *The Log* proclaimed that we were in the presence of masters of our field: Dean Wesley Clark and Professors Roland Wolseley, George Bird, Philip Ward Burton, Edmund Arnold, André Fontaine, Robert Root, William Ehling, and Catherine Covert, among others. *The Log* signified quality—and with it, respectability. It bespoke a confidence that communication was an important field whose lessons were transmitted by people who had credentials.

The Newhouse faculty had taken charge of its educational assignment in a manner that grappled successfully with the competing cultures of the university and the communication industry. There is no evidence they suffered from what scholars call *status deprivation:* falling short of the requirements of university life and being treated punitively because of it.

If *The Log* were taken at face value, the Newhouse School would have appeared to be on commanding heights of communication education. It had the best physical plant in the United States and a seemingly generous budget. My impression was that faculty members held their heads high and commanded respect in other quarters of the university as well as outside the academy. As a student in an experimental program called Mental Health Communications, funded by the National Institute of Mental Health, I frequently contacted several other university departments where I was received enthusiastically. This, I would later learn, was not always the situation elsewhere in the United States for communication, journalism, and media studies students.[3]

Later, as a faculty member at several universities, as a dean of a school of journalism, and as a president of the Association for

Education in Journalism and Mass Communication, I learned that my early experience at Syracuse was more often the exception than the rule. Journalism schools were sometimes pariahs on their campuses, and students seeking admission to advanced graduate courses elsewhere on campus were occasionally rebuffed or repelled. At Syracuse, the school of communications had status, perhaps because of its resources, given by the press lord S. I. Newhouse. Indeed, the first year I spent at Syracuse, our building was dedicated by no less a luminary than President Lyndon B. Johnson. Few schools before or since have had a presidential dedication and the instant visibility it brought.

Although I thought Syracuse somehow accommodated the professional and the scholar under the roof of an elegant I. M. Pei building, I would also learn that my school, like other such schools, lived with tensions that are part of journalism and communication education's schizophrenic state as it tries to serve two sometimes contradictory masters.

Within almost any university community one can hear occasional charges that communication has no corpus of scholarship, no body of significant research. There are rumblings about "vocationalism" and charges that the communication school is really a trade school unworthy of the academy's embrace. Some faculty members in other fields say the journalism and communication school curriculum is anti-intellectual and defensive about the sometimes questionable practices of the media. And there is the frequent query about whether study in communication deprives students of needed instruction in the liberal arts and sciences. Moreover, outside colleagues make it clear that to them the communication school is not central to the purposes of the university, arguing that many prestigious universities get along very well without them.

If the curriculum of the communication school offends some critics, so do the credentials of its faculty. Most university departments have clearly prescribed requirements for their faculty: all must have terminal degrees in the field and there is (in effect) a national norm about what professors should accomplish between initial appointment and eventual promotion and tenure. For the communication school, with its interests ranging from advertising education to newsroom preparation and communication research, the requirements are diffuse and diverse. They are harder to convey to university committees that are sometimes unsympathetic to the complexities of a communication school faculty, which must have requisite professional and academic experience to be credible. As a result, when communication faculty dossiers do not match those of people in other fields, outright rejection can result.

As if things on campus were not bad enough, the communication school is also beset with communications industry critics. "You are simply too theoretical," they say. "You don't care about newspaper production or the operational problems of a television station."[4] Thus, while campus critics often remark that communication schools are out of touch with the academy, professionals say they are not quite in touch with the "real world." Many professionals not only dislike what is taught in the communication schools—they do not much like or trust those who teach it.

Although many of these commentators offer little in the way of prescriptions to improve the enterprise, they somehow believe that the industry holds the franchise when it comes to educating people for professional careers. Unlike other fields that have happily delegated legal or business education to scholars and teachers instead of practitioners, the communication industry still harbors the belief that emulating the norm of professional practice is highly desirable. In such a world view, there is little time for critical analysis or instruction about professional ideals. Such a view relegates the communication school to the position of industry handmaiden rather than independent analyst or leader.[5] Journalism and communication schools are thus light-years from the relative maturity of schools that train future legal or business talent.

Another refrain of critics is that some media fields or subfields are not well represented in journalism and mass communication schools. In that schools of communication are umbrella agencies for the study of and training in the various media industries, they naturally have multiple constituencies. I have rarely met any newspaper editors, public relations practitioners, or advertising executives who felt that their field was well represented in existing schools. Not unusual is the complaint from professionals in the electronic media that they are grossly underrepresented in schools that have considerable loyalty to the print media.

Thus the communication school, its faculty, students, and alumni often live in a confused atmosphere beset by mixed signals, largely because they have many points of reference. The school attempts to address several constituencies, some of which are, unfortunately, at cross purposes. Purists in the academy doubt the value of professional education and suspect it is draining the liberal arts. Some industry people want professional schools to serve the world of practice, training entry-level professionals for various roles in the industry. At the same time, the broad mandate of communication schools with interests ranging from advertising to electronic media and magazine instruction (and resources) is to satisfy individual subfields as well as other constituencies.

The condition faced by individual communication educators is often one of self-doubt. They try to satisfy both the scholarly demands of the university and the practical requirements of the communication industry. To justify a place on the campus of a research university, a communication school needs to contribute to the commonweal—it must attract and keep students as well as recruit and retain a quality faculty. In that communication school, the composition of faculty is itself a complex chemistry because the school must contain people with considerable academic training and requisite professional experience. The successful professional school needs respect from its chief constituents, namely the media industries and related auxiliaries. Journalism and communication professors must necessarily be more than professionals on loan; they must also be educators with a penchant and competence for teaching, research, and public service.[6]

Thus communication professors today are faced with contradictory demands. They necessarily worry about connecting their students with a rapidly changing industry and world. At the same time, they must be productive enough to keep their jobs and earn tenure by engaging in research, scholarly work, and critical analysis. These professors are also expected to make connections with other colleagues on campus and with industry professionals. In the midst of these multiple demands, the feedback they hear is not always praise.

The origins of these contradictions and stresses are fairly clear. Unlike other professional schools, journalism and communication faculties frequently recruit to their ranks practitioners with no scholarly training. Curiously, the new faculty member from the profession is often given a tenure-track appointment with vague references to productivity and promotion "down the road." This has happened often because communication schools have been blessed (or plagued) by large enrollments that require increasing numbers of faculty, especially faculty who can teach basic professional courses.

Thus people are actively recruited from the mass media; from news organizations, and other professional settings such as advertising agencies and public relations firms. These new faculty members often face work-intensive classes and several sections of professional skills courses; there is little time for reflection or research.

But this typical scenario can be altered, as several innovative programs and administrators have demonstrated. Instead of letting a person ill suited for academic pursuits sink or swim, several universities have initiated programs of faculty development. Also, considerable aid and comfort has been provided by a joint communiqué of U.S. newspaper editors and journalism educators. In the mid-1980s the Committee on News Editorial Education, a joint venture of the American Society of Newspaper Editors and the Association for Education in Journalism and Mass Communication, issued a statement calling for a two-track approach that would seek both scholars and professionals in its faculty recruitment and hiring. Under this system, now accepted in some schools, faculty members who are hired from the traditional academic arenas are expected to obey the long-accepted rules of the academy, balancing the three-legged stool of productivity based on research, teaching, and service. Other faculty hired from the various media professions are given a different, but still rigorous, standard. Instead of writing the traditional scholarly articles and treatises, they can produce texts, essays, op-ed pieces, and other examples of professional productivity, as long as it has something to do with media studies. It cannot be mere professional work that would be done by entry-level people in the media; it must be distinguished and must contribute to knowledge and understanding.

As yet, this two-track system has not found universal acceptance in the United States. Some schools, such as Syracuse University, are carefully examining the idea as it might relate to all professional programs and not just to journalism, but it remains under discussion. It is a controversial issue on many campuses. Traditionally trained academics tend to believe, possibly with some justification, that it would institutionalize what they see as the shortcomings of professionals who are unable to conduct research or to publish in the more rigorous academic media. Others see it, again with some justification, as a means of retaining people who are genuinely needed to teach professional and career-related courses but who are unlikely to perform as conventional scholars or researchers. That is why recent efforts to recruit communication school faculty into a two-track system are especially encouraging.

The "Carey Grants," administered by Dean James W. Carey of the University of Illinois College of Communications under a recent grant from The Freedom Forum, reflect a particularly encouraging interest in journalism faculty development. These small grants are awarded to journalism and communication faculty whose projects include major books, articles, and exhibits wherein their journalistic skills are displayed. These projects, too, might well count when a person is advanced to the tenure table.

These considerations aside, I contend that any intelligent person who moves from the professional world to teaching careers in journalism can get promoted if they plan well and demonstrate their competence in acceptable ways. There are no secrets about how to do this.

First, if they do not have a dean who aids in their development, they must do it themselves. This may mean conducting research or taking courses to master the nature of scholarly inquiry. Journalism and typical media work are usually not systematic. Scholarship is. But systematic methods of scholarship can be learned, even on one's own.

Second, the professionally oriented faculty member is well advised to seek out and make use of a mentor/partner—to work collaboratively with someone who has scholarly credentials but perhaps less experience in the realities of the communication industry. This pairing is symbiotic: each can serve as a mentor/partner for the other and each can bring something of considerable value to the undertaking. In cases in which former media professionals have paired with research scholars, particularly successful teams have resulted.

Third, some schools bring together their research professors and their media professionals in specially designed workshops, organized as short-term and carefully designed minicourses focusing on specific aspects of that research process (e.g., sampling, statistical procedures, measurement). These workshops enable busy instructors to forego regular semester-long courses with students that may cover much unneeded material. This, of course, implies an administration supportive of faculty development.

Fourth, media professionals who have become professors ought to keep writing. Too many people who become journalism school faculty stop being productive professionals. While dedicating themselves to teaching and service, they can also produce articles for journalism reviews, trade publications, and other useful outlets.

Fifth, above all, they need to learn the written and unwritten "rules" of the academy—to get a full and exact understanding of what they need to do to ensure tenure and promotion, should that be the goal. The professionals may not like the requirements or they may wish they were not there, but the expectations of the academy are the realities in which they now live and serve. If they fully map out at the outset what will be required of them, there will be no unpleasant surprises at tenure time. Few people who think through, plan, and genuinely try to meet these requirements are denied tenure and promotion in the end.

I have made the critical case in this essay, but is all of this negative? Certainly not. Rather, I have tried to reflect the multiple demands of an information society in the process of redefinition. There is no consensus today about what constitutes the best type of university education, as critics such as Allan Bloom, E. D. Hirsch, Charles Sykes, and William Bennett so vividly demonstrate in the controversies they have ignited. At the same time, people within the communication industry (itself undergoing fundamental changes) can hardly know their own needs from day to day, let alone personnel requirements five or ten years hence.

Actually, the pressures on communication schools are quite flattering, although they may not always seem to be. Certainly, the extraordinary attention validates communication schools as important enterprises that are highly valued and worthy of scrutiny and debate. When communication schools established their present broad mandate, they also accepted the continuing interest and assessment of internal and external critics. It is not always a pleasant process, but it is meaningful and necessary.[7]

What should leaders of communication schools do about the cross fire from their critics? They can listen, learn, and make use of this unwanted attention for productive ends. This means being responsive citizens of the academy while also serving society's need for quality communicators. It is up to those in control of communication education, who have open doors to campus and industry colleagues, to decide what to do. There are a number of helpful guidelines. The Syracuse Experiment on reducing the boundaries between liberal and professional education is one example.[8] After all, administrators and faculty are the experts hired to conduct communication education. They ought to carry out their mission coherently and with intellectual honesty. They may want to listen to professional critics, but in the end must make their own decisions and fashion educational policies that will best serve the society and be appropriate within the role of the university.

Notes

1. From 1970 to 1988, scores of articles appeared in the popular and trade press about journalism schools, ranging from Ben Bagdikian's (1977, March) much-discussed "Woodstein U—Notes on the Mass Production and Questionable Education of Journalists," *Atlantic Monthly*, to more recent articles in the *Washington Monthly* (1986, May). The trade press (especially *Editor and Publisher* and *presstime* magazines) is also a frequent source of articles about journalism education—e.g., "Journalism Education: Storm Swirls, Changes on Campus," *presstime* (1983, September). A full issue of the *Gannett Center Journal* was devoted to this topic in Spring 1988, "The Making of Journalists." A useful intellectual critique of journalism and communication education is Stephen White's (1986, Winter) "Why Journalism Schools?" *Public Interest*, 39-57.

2. Hopkins was a clergyman and physician who served as the president of Williams College from 1857 to 1887.

3. See the critique of journalism schools' reputations in *Planning for Curricular Change in Journalism Education* (1987). (2d ed., pp. 1-2). Eugene: School of Journalism, University of Oregon; and Everette Dennis (1988, Spring). "Whatever Happened to Marse Robert's Dream?" *Gannett Center Journal*, 2-22.

4. See Everette E. Dennis (1986). "It Wouldn't Work in Theory: Overcoming Resistance to Research About the Mass Media." Clissold Lecture. University of Western Ontario, London, Ontario. (Reprinted in *Comment,* a Canadian media magazine.)

5. See George Gerbner (1984, April). "Defining the Field of Communication." *ACA Bulletin*, p. 1.

6. A useful discussion is Robert Blanchard's (1988, Autumn). "Our Emerging Role in Liberal and Media Studies: How Do We Break the News to Media Professionals?" *Journalism Educator*, 28-31.

7. For a wide-ranging view of the field see, Nancy Sharp (Ed.) (1988). *Communications Research: The Challenge of the Information Age*. Syracuse, NY: Syracuse University Press.

8. This is a review of issues and problems related to the remarkable rise in recent years of undergraduate enrollment in professional schools and the corresponding drop in enrollment in arts and sciences degree programs. Some twenty faculty members from various disciplines offer suggestions about how to reduce barriers between disciplines. (See P. March [Ed.]. [1988]. *Contesting the Boundaries of Liberal and Professional Education: The Syracuse Experiment*. Syracuse, NY: Syracuse University Press.)

15. Media Studies: Glue for the Global Village[†]

The name has changed. The mandate has not. That was the word
from our trustees when they met at the Gannett Foundation Media
Center in the fall of 1990 and shortened what had been a long and
cumbersome name. As we change our moniker from the Gannett
Center for Media Studies, a Gannett Foundation Program at Columbia University to the Gannett Foundation Media Center, we have
been asked whether this reflects any change in direction or purpose.

Anything but. When the center opened its doors in 1985, it was
designated as an "institute for the advanced study of mass communication and technological change." That is still what we are, but
there have been two significant changes. The first is the recognition,
incremental at first and later underscored by our governing body,
the Gannett Foundation trustees, and our program advisers, the
National Advisory Committee, that our work must be international
in scope, bearing witness to a field that is truly global.

The second is a renewed commitment not only to the research we
support in fellows programs, conferences, and staff work but also a
major research effort that will soon become part of our regular
operating structure.

Both of these matters were part of a five-year report on the center's
operations and are now being carried out by international fellows and
through globally oriented work in conferences, seminars and publications, as well as a much expanded in-house research capability.

Over the course of our first six years we have commissioned work
on media and the public trust, public attitudes toward the media,
the relationship between institutions and media, and a variety of
other topics. We have also developed a publications program and a
system of public scholarship wherein reporters, media critics and
others interested in information and knowledge about mass communications and technological change could be served. The result
has been various occasional papers, working papers, research reports, reprints, speeches, background papers, monographs, books,
and a quarterly journal.

---

† *Communiqué* column, December 1990 (monthly newsletter of FFMSC).

The next phase of our work here will be greater capability to engage in critical-events research (sometimes called "firehouse" studies), synthetic and analytic reports on the state of knowledge in given media arenas, as well as original "great issue" studies. As always our work is meant to expand upon and supplement that already in existence.

When it comes to media studies, there are many noteworthy enterprises and people, ranging from journalism and mass communication graduate programs to individual scholars in various university fields, think tanks, industry research organizations and elsewhere. We have surveyed this considerable work and still find that there is a special niche unfilled by others that we will continue to address.

Our dedication is to the pursuit of important questions, rigorously addressed with a variety of appropriate methods and to the readable, coherent and accessible reporting of results. This is to us what media studies is all about and it is to this endeavor that we continue our commitment. If anything, our new name more closely associates us with the nonprofit, philanthropic world in which we have always lived, but in a fashion that is open to different ways of knowing and that respects both the yield of practical experience on the one hand and systematic study on the other. It could be that this really is the glue that will hold the global village together.

16. The Smart Journalist in the Year 2000[†]

Journalism is at once the most rigorous and the most casual of professions. Some argue it is essential for intelligent journalists to know just about everything: to be a generalist's generalist, liberally educated, open-minded, untempted by easy assumptions that are not thoroughly researched and factually checked. In short, we are

---

[†] Speech originally delivered at the FFMSC's Leadership Institute in New York, June 1988. Later published as part of the 1989 APME Journalism Education Committee Report, 1989.

talking about a renaissance person in an age of specialization. Yet
there are and can be no mandated requirements for journalism. In
fact, virtually anyone who can get a job (or publish a free-lance
article) can consider oneself a journalist.

The omnicompetent person every editor wants to hire would
presumably require a rigorous, prescribed education. In fact, that
never seems to be the case. Instead, editors and other media executives speak vaguely of the liberally educated person, presuming
somehow that their editorial employees will come to their first
assignment with requisite journalistic skills and competencies that
will mature and be polished through years of experience.

Whether the ideal journalist needs a journalism education, either
at the undergraduate or master's level, is still a matter of some
debate. Nevertheless, most journalists hired by daily newspapers
(85% industry data show) do come from journalism schools. Pre-
tending that this is not the case, as some editors do, helps keep the
journalism schools "down on the farm" and contributes mightily to
the low self-esteem that some journalists have.

I am at a loss to explain why so many American editors want to
denigrate the best system of journalism education in the world
rather than help it achieve a place on the commanding heights of
the information society. But the problem is an old one, and the
prejudice against journalism school graduates persists in spite of the
reality of hiring patterns.

Any effort to define a system of education that serves people who
want to be journalists, those who will hire them, and inevitably,
society, must clear this hurdle or at least circumvent it.

That the world is changing and changing radically is recognized
by almost everyone. And surely the daily newspaper, as well as
news organizations in the electronic media, is undergoing wrenching change as the economics of communication and its attendant
technologies experience upheaval. The smart journalist who will be
both intelligent and functional in the year 2000 needs to prepare or
be prepared for these inevitabilities.

The information society means that more and more people will
be employed in knowledge industries and will themselves be information brokers in some fashion. At the same time, there will be a
convergence of media not just at the ownership level, where a typical
media company will own various print and electronic enterprises, but
at the level of the individual communication worker, who will

increasingly move betwixt and between different media organizations. Already it is not unusual for some print journalists, typically in magazines, to also make radio and television appearances and to have their work channeled into databases and other information services. The journalist of the future will probably not want to be a narrow devotee of one medium, however worthy, if he or she hopes to move from entry-level jobs into positions of leadership. Increasingly, those devoted to narrow functions within a single medium (including newspapers) will have little chance of advancement.

This is the reality of a communication system in which all media are coming together into a single, electronically based, computer-driven system. Today there are far more similarities between and across media than there are differences. Newsgathering is newsgathering, and the most progressive practitioners are as likely to be found in database companies as they are in newspapers or the more traditional electronic media.

Journalism education in the year 2000 (if indeed the term *journalism,* which is a narrow and increasingly irrelevant concept, survives) will be found in the midst of a system of higher education also undergoing continuous change and redefinition. That will involve a redefinition of the liberal arts, with the inclusion of several new fields of knowledge and the likely retirement of others. This dynamic process has already begun globally, but in a decade or so it will be in full fruition. We have already seen a return to basics, an embracing of broader ethnic and cultural studies, and quick and practical connections to professional and technical training. The nature of the essential elements of the liberal arts will be modified over time as some new fields, especially in the sciences, move into ascendancy.

Ideally, journalists and journalism educators ought to be involved in this continuing debate, but if past experience instructs at all, they probably will not. Instead they will stand on the sidelines assuming that liberal education will remain in its traditional form and that change is unthinkable. But change will come, and the decisions will probably be made, unfortunately, by educators in the traditional disciplines with little connection to what editors and journalism educators think. Thus the need for more educators to join the debate.

The problem persists with editors as well. Particularly in the 1980s, too many editors assumed that a liberal arts education was largely the same as it was when they were students. Universities and their requirements underwent considerable change after the 1960s, and this is rarely recognized by many leading journalists today. Of course, that recognition will come as the next generation of leadership moves into command.

Journalism education will survive in the next century because, despite all the grousing, it does serve the communication industry quite efficiently. Journalism schools will probably travel along one of three tracks: some will hue to a traditional line—teaching mainly writing, reporting, and editing along a medium-specific track committed mainly to newspapers and electronic media; another cluster of schools will be umbrella organizations for various industry interests, including the news media, advertising, public relations, and others with some connecting scholarship but with little integration. A third cluster will be information-society schools connected in a holistic fashion to media studies and with-professional tracks for future industry professionals. If there is a fourth cluster, it will be much more theoretical than the other three and essentially indistinguishable from courses and concentrations in social science and humanities departments that encourage generic examinations of media studies.

Just how the smart journalist of the future uses higher education to prepare for a life and career in the field can be encouraged or deterred by the structure of higher education, whether in the liberal arts college generally or in a professional or scholarly school of journalism. Beyond the university's role, however, expect to see continued growth of industry-sponsored early-and mid-career training programs, both in-house and between media industries. In addition, various educational institutions from think tanks and media studies centers to resourceful and entrepreneurial schools will try to fill the gap between university-level preparation at either the undergraduate or graduate level, and the realities of life in the business.

The intelligent journalist will try to acquire both basic education and professional training that will make for functional participation in the work force of newspapers and electronic media organizations. This means:

- A general education as it is defined by the contemporary university system.
- Substantive specialized knowledge in one or two fields, typically a traditional academic field in the arts or sciences.
- Literacy—both traditional verbal literacy and visual literacy.

- Fundamental skills essential to one's chosen field, which may include computer literacy.
- Connectedness—the ability to synthesize and make sense of the world by connecting different fields of knowledge.
- Context—involving an integration of different ways of knowing and systems of knowledge.
- International understanding—a sense of the global nature of the modern world across all fields of knowledge.

Journalists who trek into the communication industries will then as now be able to survive by their wits and their ability to be quick studies. The more intelligent journalist will need:

Basic skills, either learned on the job or in the classroom, including journalistic writing, information-gathering, editing, and others.
Substantive knowledge about the role of journalism and communication in the larger communication environment, including some acquaintance with the history, economics, sociology, politics, and philosophy of media.
Versatility, including the ability to be flexible in the modern media environment, working in more than one medium, and adapting to changing market conditions and needs.

It is mastery of the second and third points here that will help determine whether the journalist of the future plays a leadership role in the media industries or is simply a hod carrier who works for MBA-trained managers who do know how to apply their skills in broad-gauged fashion.

As always, the institution of journalism education can only provide cues to the individual. It can mislead and erect barriers, or it can give the student a passport to the information society by pushing beyond narrow perspectives and considering the changing role of the news media in a dynamic information environment.

This means that the ideal journalism school of the future will not be a journalism school in the conventional sense at all. It will be well integrated into the life of the university, not a separate "poor cousin," as many schools are today. It will contribute to general education of all students as well as serving its own. It will use technology to liberalize its students and connect them with the information riches of the university. It will demand the best in written, oral, and visual expression, while fostering ideas and creative thinking. It will tell them that there is a powerful legacy of thoughtful media scholarship,

and great classics that all intelligent journalists should read or at
least know about. It will teach its students not to make unwarranted
assumptions, but to pursue information and knowledge systematically. Perhaps most important, it will inculcate in them a mechanism
for intellectual growth and understanding so that their knowledge
will not be out-of-date five years after they graduate.

Most progressive journalism schools in the next century will
foster leadership qualities by offering educational passports to other
fields with pride and powerful involvement, not as supplicants who
have nothing themselves to contribute.

It is my guess that there will be relatively few of the schools I am
describing, but they will be highly competitive and the best and
brightest will seek places in them. In time, they will foster change
and risk-taking among their peers.

To date, only a few journalism schools and other media institutions
have given more than lip service to the physical and philosophical
changes that are sweeping society and media. They cling, not inappro-
priately, to old values and resist trendy changes. Often, however, they
fail to catch the drift of basic societal changes that demand a response.

The jury is still out as to whether journalism schools will be
important or peripheral in the next century. I hope they will be
important, but recognize that it will not happen without gifted
leadership and dedicated work. It will be necessary to embrace
change and advance the cause of communication by being consum-
mate contemporaries while still holding basic values that assure
continued devotion to free expression.

17. Doctoral Education: A Well-Kept Secret[†]

Although virtually every journalism school in the United States
employs faculty members who have doctorates in mass communi-

---

† Speech given at the Association of Schools of Journalism and Mass Communication, "Doctoral Education May Be Our Best-Kept Secret," July 2, 1988, Portland,
Oregon.

cation, these academic degrees and the programs that produce them are not often discussed or well understood by anyone who is not a card-carrying member of this exclusive priesthood.

Doctoral programs in journalism and mass communication are our field's best kept secret. They are among the most rigorous Ph.D. programs in American universities. They have considerable utility not only for journalism schools but also for other university departments in which media studies are once again in vogue. They can also benefit the media industries, which need high-level talent, especially in research and strategic planning.

Just what is a doctoral education in mass communication? It is at once a mastery of the literature of mass communication—which has a considerable corpus these days—and specialization in one or more subject areas, such as communication history or law, media sociology or others. It is also education at the highest level of scholarship, wherein methodological skill in such areas as survey research, content analysis, critical studies, or others is part of the regimen. Of course doctoral students in mass communication do a substantial amount of work outside their own home department or school in such fields as psychology, sociology, political science, law, business, and others. They take up the subject matter of mass communication and its methodological tools as well as the substance of collateral fields. This is a demanding educational experience, one that requires considerable intellectual and professional versatility by the student. At most universities that offer it, the Ph.D. in mass communication is much more rigorous than doctorates in many other fields. It requires expansive knowledge of mass communication, interdisciplinary connections, and competence in the tools of scholarship. Far from conjecture on my part, these observations are made on the basis of comparing requirements in other fields and comments from colleagues in other disciplines. "I think you people overcompensate," a political scientist once told me. "You and your colleagues sometimes overkill on methodology and advanced statistics. We're more relaxed about this," he said. Part of this "overkill" of both substance and method springs from a desire to make the doctorate in mass communication as rigorous as possible and to gain respectability among other advanced degree programs.

Nearly twenty years ago, as a potential consumer of doctoral education, I first explored the nation's twenty-plus doctoral programs in communication and discovered one of the best-kept secrets in American higher education. When it comes to doctoral education, people's feelings about it are pretty close to the surface. There is rarely a need or desire to evaluate the Ph.D. in any comparative or contextual sense. To some, the Ph.D. is a union card essential for a tenure track appointment at a research university. To others, it is a point of entry for a life of the mind in media studies where systematic inquiry is enhanced by study at the doctoral level. Still others say a doctorate is superfluous, a pretentious exercise of no particular value to the school, its students, or the media.

I had little notion of what Ph.D.'s in mass communication were all about when I wrote to those twenty-plus schools and asked for their catalogues. After reviewing these materials I wrote to several acquaintances who held recent doctorates from about ten different schools. I considered their assessments and then visited eight programs, where I talked to administrators, faculty, and graduate students. I wanted to know what the requirements were, the nature of the course work both within the world of journalism and outside it. I wanted to know about faculty members I would likely work with—their attainment and current research interests. I also wanted to know something about the track record of the school's graduates—whether they finished or not and where they were working. And like so many older graduate students, I wanted to find a program where I could get the best possible education in the least amount of time.

Since then, of course, I have been conscious of doctoral programs, both those with long traditions and those recently established. And to the extent that we can generalize about them, I believe that doctoral programs in mass communication have more than established their place in American higher education. There are still relatively few programs—about two dozen—associated with schools of journalism or communication emphasizing media studies. There are a variety of others in speech-communication departments, which have a different mandate. Generally they have high standards—sometimes much higher than other social science and humanities fields—and are proud of the rigor of their requirements.

These programs have enormous diversity, although all of them share a common literature. Most of them are conceptually based—as opposed to professionally oriented master's programs—and demand that their students master the literature of the field as the individual school defines it. They are also expected to learn methods of scholarly inquiry, ranging from empirical analysis to documentary study. The diversity of these programs is both a virtue and a vice. Some practice a kind of substantive and methodological fascism, so narrow and restricted are accepted topics and tools. Others have a "Lazy Susan" approach to media studies, claiming to be home to every subject and method imaginable. These are the programs that say they offer both qualitative and quantitative approaches, and can do history, law, international communication, media sociology, and economics, theory and methods, and much more—all with a faculty of five! The truly competent program is somewhere in between these two extremes, doing what is appropriate based on faculty strength and expertise. I am wary of programs that try to do too much or of new programs that clone approaches developed in other places with little local context or justification. We should remember that most doctoral programs in the field are idiosyncratic and grew out of the intellectual soil of a particular community. They are strongly related to established faculty interests in a given school and the supporting environment of the larger university.

Mass communication doctoral programs are better than many people realize. There are few doctoral programs in the field that are really well-known on their own campuses. Ask historians or sociologists at many major universities to describe and assess the mass communication doctoral program on their campus and they are stumped. They may be positively or negatively inclined, but chances are they do not know much about it, what the requirements are and how it compares with other Ph.D. programs in related fields. Indeed, some programs are not even well-known in their own departments and schools. In many places a relatively few faculty members minister to the needs of the doctoral program, and they do little to explain and interpret this work to their colleagues.

If doctoral programs are poorly understood on their own campuses, it is no wonder they are neither well-known nor respected in the media industries. Reaction to the field, as I have seen it, ranges from amused tolerance to contempt. For those in the media industries who have examined the rigorous requirements of these degrees and the depth of study they offer, respect comes easily. This is especially true when doctoral research investigates important problems and questions—and is well written. The key to real world respect is linked to the pertinence of research to worthy issues and problems. This usually requires sound interpretation and explanation, as much doctoral-level research is often quite complex. Some of it is highly theoretical and wins outside respect for its rigor and hard thought, whether relevant in the short run or not. I would be the first to say that the doctoral dissertations need not to be aimed at media professionals, but where possible, they ought to be explained and interpreted for the broadest possible audience that can benefit from their findings. Highly theoretical work in media studies cannot be expected to have any more lay or professional takers than similar work in mathematics or physics, of course.

Although most media professionals do not seek out Ph.D.'s when they do recruiting, there may be more opportunities in the management of media organizations. In an era when audience research is being redefined by technology and economics, people with research training are much needed. So much the better that they have a penchant for the communication field, unlike, say, market researchers out of business schools or sociologists with little or no interest in media. We should not forget that Frank Stanton, *Doctor* Frank Stanton, who served as president of the entire CBS Network, had a Ph.D. in industrial psychology, but thought of himself as a communications researcher. Now that is a success story!

As we look toward the next century, where can we expect the graduates of mass communication doctoral programs to be employed? Then, as now, I suspect, universities will make the first claim on the hearts and minds of newly minted Ph.D.'s. However, for those who want alternative careers, research both in the media industries and elsewhere in the private sector will have allure. There is a continuing need, not just for market research, but for audience and organizational study of all types. Such researchers are hired now, but far too few come from doctoral programs in mass communication, which are often not known to those doing the hiring. That should be corrected.

Beyond the research department, media industries will probably do more of their own in-house education and training. They have special needs that cannot (and probably should not) be carried out by universities. Also in the private sector, Ph.D.'s in mass communication ought to become part of strategic planning departments. Similar opportunities are also evident in the public sector. Positions for doctorate holders in government may have diminished in recent years, but if we are to believe Arthur M. Schlesinger Jr., we will again see the cycles of history turn, with Washington and state capitals seeking the kind of expertise that doctoral graduates can provide.

The world of foundations—the independent sector—not large when compared to the private sector or government, can also employ doctoral graduates in programming, planning, and research.

The cheerful future and substantial demand for Ph.D.'s in mass communication is predicated, of course, on several assumptions. I assume that the programs now in existence and others to be developed will maintain the same high quality and competitive edge they have had in the past. This means that the Ph.D. will have "value added" both for the individual seeking it as well as for the institution employing that person. Programs must continue to be useful as well as pertinent to media and society needs. They must also be rigorous, demanding, and hard thought from their students, guaranteeing both wide-ranging knowledge and competence in research. Also, they must be comprehensive, giving their students some context for communication vis-à-vis other fields while insisting that they master its contours. Finally, the best programs must be distinctive. They will carry the special mark of their institutions and their faculty.

America's journalism and communication schools have benefitted from a trained professorate for many years. Early faculty members often took their doctorates in the social sciences, while more recently they have relied on doctorates in mass communication. Of course the mass communication Ph.D.'s co-exist with faculty members who have experience in the media and less in the way of academic credentials. Much has been written about the virtue of bringing faculty members from industry to the academy, and a joint effort of the Association for Education in Journalism and Mass Communication and the American Society of Newspaper Editors has given considerable aid and comfort to such an enterprise. Much less has and is being said about doctoral education, which when combined with some serious acquaintance with the media, is especially suited for careers in education that require a capacity for teaching and research as well as knowledge of the literature of journalism, mass communication, and media studies. The doctorate is more than a union card, it is the essential ingredient for those who choose the university life, who want to contribute to knowledge and to teach with systematic connections to the academy and the field of communication itself.

On the Consequences
of Convergence

18. What You Don't Know Can Hurt You[†]

There is, of course, nothing new about the concept that information is power, something evident to Greek and Roman generals on their respective battlefields centuries ago. So, we might ask, why talk about the utility and economic virtue of information? Is it not all pretty obvious?

At one level, the answer is yes, the value and importance of information are obvious. But at another level the sources, contours, uses, and economic impact of information are anything but obvious. It is a complex subject, one only now evolving into a coherent enterprise and field of interest. Still, there is something new about the accelerating avalanche of information made possible by the massive information, storage and retrieval capabilities of the computer. And there is something thoughtfully refreshing in Harlan Cleveland's notion that "information is a renewable resource," one that will increasingly play a central role in our economy.

Only recently have we as a society become self-conscious about the role, function, and future of information. For those in business, the growing impact of information in an information economy is a well-established reality. The notion that not knowing something could be harmful takes me back to a courtroom in Chicago in the 1960s, where I saw a gentlemanly old lawyer urge the court to dismiss on summary judgment a pending case, relying on a well-tested statute. Opposing counsel smiled and revealed that the statute had been overruled by the state supreme court only a week earlier. The case continued and the old lawyer's client eventually lost, hampered by poor preparation and misinformation.

I cite this case because lawyers were far ahead of all of us, even without the computer, in fashioning a rigorous and reliable system of storing information and knowledge. But even that excellent system

† Speech delivered at a conference of the Western Council of State Libraries, "What You Don't Know Can Hurt You: Considerations About Information in the Information Society," December 1989, Keystone Resort, Colorado.

was only as good as its users. We can all recall stories of instances in which incomplete, inaccurate, or incompetent information-gathering made a difference to a business transaction, a legal ruling, or a personnel decision. In the field of journalism, there are so many instances in which inadequate information misinforms or misleads the public that there would not be time to retrieve them even if we were to develop an electronic menu for that purpose. A good example of this is the 1981 case of "Jimmy's World," the story of a child drug addict that ran in the *Washington Post* and which was later discovered to be completely fabricated by the reporter, Janet Cooke. Her inventive story won the Pulitzer Prize before it was revealed that Jimmy was not a single character, but rather a composite of many. There was misrepresentation of information at several levels, proving that even a respected newspaper with a fairly rigorous system of checking could be fooled.

In a reversal of T. S. Eliot's classic formulation, we know that data need analysis and human connection to become information, that there is a considerable distance between information and knowledge, let alone knowledge and wisdom. Thus we need more than a recitation of the truism that information is power and that not having it can put all of us at a considerable disadvantage in a society more and more reliant on information for transactions, from the most mundane to the most critical.

These issues raise four important questions: (a) Who will provide information? And what are their purposes and values? (b) How will institutions use that information and to what purpose? (c) How will people learn to exercise quality control over information? and (d) Who will own, exploit, and recycle information to the benefit of themselves or society?

Information Creators and Providers

At the moment, several critical institutions are essential information providers, and each has its own vested interests. These information providers have both separate and overlapping identities and purposes. The three principal institutions in this battle over information are business, government, and universities. There are, of course, other entities, such as foundations and nonprofit organizations of the independent sector; the military, actually a subset of government; and the media or communications industry, which is generally a part of business. Librarians are and will continue to play a key role in each of these institutions as they access, process, and disseminate information. Anyone gathering or using information has to be well aware of the purposes for which information is gathered, acquired, processed, and disseminated.

Without suggesting nefarious intent, we must recognize that information is not a neutral commodity but one shaped, framed, and presented for specific purposes. In business, for example, the new and developing field of business information which grew into an enterprise with $15 billion in annual spending in the United States alone by 1992. Business has made it clear that it needs timely, specialized information not readily available from public sources in order to function effectively. With the help of technology and variable channels for distribution, a demand has been created for business information services. This includes intelligence about general business, consumer credit, market research, financial markets, regulatory affairs, accounting, and law, to name the major categories of this new and growing enterprise. The emphasis is on accurate, technical information that allows businesses—giant and tiny—to conduct their affairs knowledgeably in an effort to maximize profits and beat the competition. Such information ranges from highly complex and calibrated material about the futures market to modest databases that help people use rental cars to find their way from the airport to their hotel courtesy of a handy printout.

Business information is jealously guarded and shared only with those willing to pay the freight, although, except in instances of industry secrets or trade protectionism, business information is generally available to all inquiries that can meet the asking price. Inquisitive persons or organizations without adequate resources need not apply for this increasingly valuable yield.

Closely connected to business information is the growing newsletter industry, which reported sales of nearly $7 billion in 1989. In a few years this industry grew from only a few publications to thousands. The field even has its own newsletter on newsletters, which nurtures entrepreneurs who want to start newsletters, typically courtesy of desktop publishing and the electronic revolution. Of course, all this suggests limitations on business information.

A case in point: While researching the history of editorial cartoons, I once visited the firm Art Instruction, Inc. in Minneapolis.

This is the correspondence school that promoted the "Draw Me Girl" on matchbook covers in the 1960s. The school once had on its staff famous comic artists like Charles Schultz and various well-known editorial cartoonists. When I asked to see the school's archives and records in the process of my work, the president, a former FBI agent, laughed, and said, "You have to understand, this is a business, not a library or museum." The records and a fine collection of commercial and comic art had all been disposed of years before. Clearly, information without an immediate pay-off or a clearly profitable use now will probably not be saved or much valued.

This brings us to government information. A few years ago one of our senior fellows at the Gannett Center, a distinguished Boston editor, and I received a briefing from a reference librarian at Columbia University. The editor asked about the range and extent of government information, and the librarian replied, "We used to have this information, but recently the government stopped publishing it, pushing that function off to a private vendor." To my untrained ear that sounded like a pretty mundane statement, but to the editor it was something else. "That's a political statement, isn't it?" he asked. And, with that, the librarian shifted gears and launched into a discussion of the Reagan administration's cutbacks on government information. This conversation led to news stories in several newspapers.

We all know that government information is collected with some respect for traditions going back to the early censuses. But it is also extended or attenuated by the weighted interests of particular administrations. Government information, while sometimes seemingly neutral, can be the most political of information, from labor force data to the consumer price index. Here is a case in which the release, timing, and packaging of information makes the difference. What it says and how it is used is part of the political process, a competition of interests that seek to solidify and expand their power. Sometimes this is done with subtlety, sometimes not. Although our complex system of government information and documentation may seem rather benign, be assured that it is not. Some information is collected, some is not. Depending on what it is and who controls it, it is easily accessible or difficult to pry loose even by legions of lawyers.

We see this more dramatically when we step outside our own system and observe the role of government information in the Soviet Union, where, thanks to Glasnost and Perestroika, its role, nature, and uses are changing dramatically and to the great confusion of many people. Traditionally, the press and the government have not been distinguishable. From the beginning of the Soviet state, the press has been an integral part of government propaganda. Now the news that the Soviet people are getting is changing dramatically. It is more candid, even critical about topics once taboo. This means essential changes in the definition of news and information and changes in the roles of journalists and other information workers. The Soviet Union is a fascinating case study of the role of information in a society where change is no longer sluggishly incremental, but bold and dramatic. Of course, whether the Soviet Union becomes an information society in the Western sense will be determined by many factors, among them technology and a working telephone system.

In the face of international competitiveness, expect government information to be much more difficult to access in the years ahead, increasingly subject to legal or technological limitations. This may not be a matter of bureaucrats hoarding information but rather a problem of knowing how to effectively retrieve the information we need.

As we consider the essentially self-serving, self-perpetuating nature of information from business and government, it seems to me that we must plead with universities to guard jealously their independence and impartiality in conducting research and disseminating results, which ought to be as close to pure and refined information as possible.

Besides the question of the quality of our information, there is the issue of how to address its gaps. For example, there is not much children's programming to begin with, and very little reliable research—business is not providing it—and government is not supporting much of it. Only the university researcher with modest funding from private foundations is generating disciplined intelligence on a subject that is compelling for anyone who is a parent, teacher, or citizen. In the midst of a critique of education that scorns research and elevates only the teaching role of higher education, we are losing sight of what A. Bartlett Giamatti called "a free and ordered space." Giamatti saw the university as a kind of protected "conversation," one that generates information and understanding on behalf of the public. As he put it: "It is a constant conversation between young and old, between students, among faculty, between faculty and students; a conversation between past and present, a conversation the culture has with itself on behalf of the country."

By asking questions important in the generation of knowledge, by rigorous methods of research and analysis, the university can, if it chooses, do what no other social entity can—pursue truth without regard to special interests or the immediate usefulness of the result. In this sense the university is a special kind of knowledge factory. Consider the kind of survey results that the best of university opinion research laboratories provide as opposed to private sector audience researchers or those commissioned by government. Because research of all kinds can be an instrument of power, as Leo Bogart has written eloquently, we need to be clear on the nature, purposes, and expected uses that research will have. Though there is quality research that generates information in the public and private sectors, universities still have the best opportunity to be courageously impartial in seeking and disseminating information.

That is why we should all worry when a research-basher like Charles Sykes makes a fine case for "Know-Nothingism" in his book *ProfScam*, wherein a research-oriented faculty are blamed for the ills of higher education. To my mind there is too little research being done by too few people, not the reverse, as Sykes argues. I worry that public and private universities are becoming so dependent on business to fund research, endow professorships, create new programs, and erect buildings that they may be bargaining away their essential independence unless safeguards are consciously established. The same might be said about the way state universities slavishly pander to public opinion, even when doing so compromises their essential purposes and independence. Information generated by universities is absolutely essential to the informed citizen, because the uninformed society is also the most fragile.

Business will, for its own economic reasons, generate information of value to the instant marketplace, if not to posterity. Governments will rightly abide by the voice of their constituents, worrying more about the present than the future. Only the university can be the timeless defender of knowledge and information that will make sense out of social change with ample considerations for the past, the present, and the future. But that is only if universities reclaim the territory that has historically been theirs.

A Place for the Press

As a student of communication, I would be remiss if I did not make a special plea for the role of the press in our system of free expression and freedom of information. Although mostly a part of the private sector (public broadcasting is one exception), the press has an obligation to its owners to survive, to make money, but it also has a social obligation, constitutionally protected, to serve the public interest by advancing the free flow of information and opinions. That latter consideration—opinion—will continue to be important in the days ahead as communication policymakers again consider what may seem at first a parochial dispute between phone companies and newspapers over electronic yellow pages.

The telephone companies say they have a right to develop this aspect of the information business without governmental restrictions. Newspaper publishers say electronic yellow pages will so erode classified advertising as a source of revenue that some newspapers may not survive, or at least not as strong economic entities. I have no doubt that modern information technologies have the wherewithal to provide the consumer with vital and important information, but I also worry that these same technologies are as yet incapable of assuming the opinion function of communication, so long a central feature of the print media. Considering what media in this country are most important in fostering the exchange of opinion, only newspapers, magazines, and books belong at the head of the class. Television has been a great disappointment in this realm, and talk radio is a primitive instrument still more often in the province of demagoguery. Electronic databases as yet do not function as members of the opinion-making media.

This is only one example of our lack of clear communication policy in the United States. We may be the only industrial democracy without such a policy or even a mechanism for establishing one. Several proposals have been made for communication policy in recent years, including a series of studies commissioned by the Markle Foundation and a creative notion advanced by attorney Stuart Brotman in a publication of the Washington Annenberg Program that calls for a council of communications advisers. All this is beyond the scope of this essay, but it is something we must keep in mind as we consider the nature of information and its sources.

Information Consumers

Inherent in any discussion of information providers is a consideration of information users. We do need a clearer conception of who information users are, whether individuals or institutions. We must ask what their needs are, what is already being provided and what is not. We need to know and understand a great deal more about how business and government get and use information. This is a target of serious study for information scientists and other scholars who care about the diffusion of knowledge, information and data. I am sometimes astonished at how primitive is the flow of information within some of our country's largest businesses. What the CEO knows (or does not know) is linked to the kind of internal and external information resources policy set up and integrated into the firm. Businesses and governments need to be self-conscious about information—what is available, what needs to be gathered, and how to disseminate it to managers, administrators, and workers. Of course, the institutional demands for information will determine what information is gathered, processed, and retrieved. Because this is so, we need, especially in our libraries and library schools, to think systematically about what information is not valued, especially in the short run, even though it may be vital over time.

Access and Understanding

The matter of just how people will learn to access and make thoughtful use of information is a subject rarely addressed. Few in American universities seem to care much about this, assuming, of course, that classical liberal arts education provides the grist for information gathering and integration. That, however, is not the case. Just as the traditional English department taught writing (when it did) by reading great literature, it never taught students how to get and process information. Presumably that is the job of every discipline, every field of study. But when we consider how many really do this, especially at the undergraduate level, it is clear we need some kind of public policy to see that this happens.

Studies show that most educated Americans do not know how to gather information in any systematic and reliable way, let alone integrate it effectively for their own purposes. We need a national commitment to teach all Americans—those in school and those long removed from the educational system—the strategies and skills necessary to get the information they need to be informed and effective citizens. This should be done by the schools at the earliest age possible and reinforced constantly by the mass media, which ought to be accessible and understandable information resources for all of our citizens.

Finally, a few words about the greatest battleground in the information society—that of the economics of information. We have not yet established effective economic or legal principles from which we can resolve essential issues of information ownership. Just what information is public, owned by the government, and by extension, all citizens, what is properly the province of the private sector and what ought to be accessible to anyone who seeks it out, is not yet certain. This is another area in which thoughtful scholars, professionals, and decision makers need to consider the public interest as it pertains to information policy. It is time we stopped pretènding that this critical concept defies definition and some degree of operationalism and work to fashion some rules that advance the public interest in the generation and use of information.

In the 1990s we can expect various interests—some of them quite self-serving—to cope with the information war, to determine who will have access to any and all information, and who will be hampered and limited. In these coming days information will no longer be an abstract term, but an economic and social reality understood and eloquently articulated for all of the people and their interests. Those who are motivated to be on the commanding heights of the information society will be there because they know, understand, and appreciate information as a renewable resource.

19. Communication and Human Frailties[†]

Hundreds, perhaps thousands, of messages about the Salman Rushdie affair have crisscrossed the world since the late Ayatollah Ruhollah Khomeini issued his death decree in reaction to Rushdie's book, *The Satanic Verses*. Yet despite the speed of modern communication, the response in the West, where one would have expected ringing declarations about freedom of expression, was painfully slow.

[†] *Communiqué* column, March 1989 (monthly newsletter of FFMSC).

Ironically, in many parts of the Third World, especially in Islamic countries where the communication infrastructure is frail, there were riots, demonstrations, and roars of vengeance. News about the Rushdie book—particularly the Ayatollah's grandstanding threat—moved with dispatch. It was received, comprehended and acted upon even by people of limited literacy and educational experience.

In the modern information societies the message traveled with the same speed, but the response was slower, more ambiguous, cautious, even among people who pride themselves on their adherence to the enlightened principles of free speech and press.

Except for the British government and the new director-general of UNESCO, there were few voices that came immediately to the defense of freedom of expression.

The initial response of many American booksellers was later recanted, but its impact was extraordinary. Book publishers initially maintained a steely silence while authors reacted slowly. The U.S. Department of State expressed tepid disapproval, and the president spoke out only in response to a direct question about Khomeini's decree at a press conference.

It was as though the principles of modern risk management played a greater role than ideas about free speech and the free flow of information. The unparalleled tools of modern communication might as well have been replaced by quill pens and diplomatic pouches, so slow and measured was the response of the two institutions in our society with the greatest responsibility for assuring free expression and the greatest vested interest in it—government and the mass media.

Governments by their nature usually consider the consequences of their actions, whether diplomatic, political, or economic. That is quite appropriate in many instances, and it is understandable that there should have been some serious thought given to the handling of the Rushdie affair.

In the end, though, we might have expected a more impassioned statement that would let the world know just where we stood on such a fundamental concern. However, the Constitution that our leaders are sworn to uphold does not say anything about timetables or scheduling.

If government has the legal responsibility to defend our freedoms, the media—the print and broadcasting press as well as book publishers and other communication outlets—have a moral responsibility to defend them. But with the Rushdie affair many in the communication industries were also slow to react. Some of them may have measured risks while others were simply preoccupied with other matters.

The news media did an extraordinarily good job covering the story, examining the issue and its complexity. In their opinion functions they were a bit ahead of their brethren in the book publishing industry, but few editorials or columns stood out as being particularly persuasive or courageous.

If nothing else the Rushdie affair provides a lesson for future reference. Some freedoms should not to be subjected to the contingencies of risk management. As Justice Hugo Black used to say, expression ought to be absolute.

Moreover it should be a reminder that something happened in America in February 1989 that no mean-spirited prosecutor or know-nothing school board could have gotten away with. As a society we flinched and, for a short time, succumbed to terrorism, but the experience gave us a short glimpse of the human factor in modern communication.

Satellites, computers, and fax machines may have brought us the global village Marshall McLuhan used to extol, but we are still and may always be subject to the human frailties that govern our response.

It has often been said that technology can enhance freedom and make possible the flow of messages with important content and visual force in a fashion heretofore unimagined. That is true, but it is also true that every link in the communication process must have a like-minded commitment to freedom. Otherwise, the chain is broken and we lose our franchise.

The Rushdie affair shook our constitutional faith as no court, public official, or powerful private interest could have. We need to take steps to prevent such a breakdown in the future.

20. Convergence and Communication Education[†]

After decades of false starts, broken promises, and deferred dreams, we have at last entered into the information society. Though

---

[†] Speech delivered at the Conference on Leadership in Communication, "Technological Convergence and Communication Education," November 15, 1989, San Diego State University, California.

superannuated futurists often overanticipated the pace and impact of technology, many of their prognostications did become reality, so much so that today it is no longer proper to speak of a communication revolution: It is now more of an evolution, moving incrementally from new inventions, innovations, and improvements to actual applications in the home or office.

The period we are talking about is characterized by rapid technological growth and perhaps more important, convergence of communication technologies.

More than 20 years ago industry analysts predicted there would be a nearly universal integration of systems that retrieve, process, and store text, data, sound, and image. They correctly predicted that this would be a time when communication and computer technologies would be converging and integrating. These developments made possible technology that was smaller and more portable, cheaper and more user-friendly. We quickly experienced a world in which television sets began to talk to computers and when all forms of communication seemed to come together in one electronically based, computer-driven system. We would talk realistically about a united state of media in which different instruments of communication had more in common than they had differences.

Those of us who were dedicated to careers in newspapers, broadcasting, or telecommunication soon learned that all of this had implications for us in the workplace, in our organizations, and in society. Critics who in the 1960s or 1970s scorned the notion that computers would ever have anything to do with newspaper reporters, copy editors, or ad salespersons were eventually to find instead that they had direct and important connections to their work. I recall once thinking that the latest computer had as much interest for me as the latest printing press had had in the 1960s, but, like others, I was mistaken.

By no means am I a technological determinist, for it is clear that technologies often appear long before they are practical, sometimes impeded more by human factors than by glitches in the lab. Those human factors include economics and politics, among others. If there is no market for a new technology, it does not succeed. If other industries and interests fearful of a new development thwart its growth, it may not be heard of again for decades. If government, whether through regulation, statute or executive order is not friendly to a new technology, it may similarly be sidetracked.

We must keep these factors in mind when any new technology arises. Some analysts do not take a new media technology seriously until it has the capacity to reach 50% of the population. However, such a formulation is now hopelessly outdated due to the rise of market segmentation and targeted communication, in which the nature and quality of the audience and its demographics are more important than sheer size. Nevertheless, we are well counselled by communication scholar John Carey, who reminds us that the newspaper took 100 years to reach the magic 50% figure; the telephone, 70 years; radio, only about 10 years; and television less than that. Cable, by contrast, was a long dormant technology for a variety of economic and regulatory reasons and took nearly 40 years to achieve 50% penetration in American households.

As we stand back to look at the contours of what the communications age has wrought, we note that communication, once a mostly nation-bound concept with national newspapers and broadcast systems, is increasingly global. Not only do messages move easily across national boundaries—witness, for example, the remarkable use of facsimile during the Chinese student revolution in the summer of 1989—but media enterprises themselves are now more likely to be global, not only in their mandate and impact but also in their ownership.

What I am talking about is the growth of giant, global media companies in this country and elsewhere, companies that own newspapers and broadcast stations, cable systems, book publishers, business information services, and other media. As media have experienced massive growth and greater global identity, their functions in this world of convergence have also begun to blur and merge in ways that are sometimes fascinating, sometimes disturbing. For example, much of the debate over television today has to do with the blurring of information and entertainment, information and opinion, and all functions with marketing and advertising. We can no longer easily tell whether a television program is information or entertainment or even whether it is simply a long, paid commercial.

Ironically, especially given its age as a medium, the newspaper industry was one of the first to get self-conscious about the meaning of convergence. In the 1970s, when American newspapers were losing both circulation and market penetration, that industry engaged in a large-scale readership project with cooperation from associations of publishers and editors as well as individual owners and groups. At stake was the very future of the newspaper. Thanks to thoughtful research and the computer, a diagnosis was prepared and a plan put into effect. This plan involved a reconsideration of newspaper content, reformatting of a traditional medium with special sections, graphics, and color. There were even new forms of writing and a redefinition of news that allowed much more material, once thought too soft or superficial to be included in the content of the newspaper, to draw new readers, among them the young.

Convergence, of course, is a coming together of the ways and means of communication, from message formation and processing to dissemination and storage. In today's world there is not much difference at either the abstract or operations level between a newspaper, a television station, a database, and a telephone system. What is different is human intention and purpose of communication. At a 1990 Gannett Center seminar, a top executive for Time Inc. (now Time Warner) was asked by a person interested in magazines to describe his company succinctly. With a bit of understatement, he said, "I guess you could say we are a cable company with some publishing interests." When asked who the company's competitors were, he did not mention *Newsweek* or the Washington Post Company, but instead the German conglomerate Bertelsmann, the French giant Hachette S.A., Rupert Murdoch's News Corporation and ABC/ Capital Cities. When the questioner persisted that all this "highfalutin" corporate talk had no meaning for individuals in media careers, the executive disagreed, saying he could foresee a time when a young person would be hired to work on *Sports Illustrated*, do assignments for *Sports Illustrated for Kids*, have their material sold to an online database, appear occasionally on radio and television talking about their work, and perhaps, even make movie deals! Now that is what we are talking about when we speak of convergence.

From this executive's comments, it is clear that convergence is occurring at the level of media functions and product development, at the level of ownership and control, in management and supervision, and with regard to individuals in the work place. It certainly suggests that educators and their students need to know and understand the concept of convergence and what it means for them personally and for communication education. I am not suggesting radical curricular reform or firing our present faculties and replacing them with information society specialists, but I am suggesting that communication education does need a strategy for coping with change in the years ahead.

To me, the lessons of convergence are quite clear. There is now more than ever a need for communication and journalism educators to cooperate with one another. Instead of building walls around programs, sequences, special interests, and individual media, this is the time to join forces, to exploit common interests rather than accentuate differences.

First, there should be an end to territorial attacks among newspaper, broadcasting, advertising, or public relations interests, whose purposes are often advanced without regard to the lessons of convergence. There is enough common ground between all forms of information acquisition, processing and storage that the pursuit of differences will clearly hurt the field. People in fields like management information systems in business schools and information science in library schools understand this. Communication educators should, too—especially by marshalling forces to generate resources and better serve our students, our scholarly interests, the communication industry and, most importantly, the public.

Of course, the idea of cooperation for mutual self-interest is not easily accomplished. Many educators and professionals are extremely parochial in their outlook, sometimes for good reasons, and are hostile to any notion of convergence even though it is now central to communication itself.

Second, communication educators should move with dispatch to determine what knowledge, information, and skills are essential to all competent students of communication, regardless of the field they will enter. Our students need a conceptual map of the information society and they also need specific knowledge and skills to be competent, productive citizens and professionals. I refer here to the core of communication, media studies, and journalism curriculum. Those who argue for narrow specialization ought to heed a recent study by Lee Becker of Ohio State University that indicates that undergraduate specialization in communications often has little to do with a student's eventual career choices. The Becker study, for example, found advertising majors who became newspaper reporters, thus challenging very seriously the narrow and parochial call of those who want to build walls around such media and individual support systems. We need more attention paid to common elements and interests in a manner that links such study and experience directly to specialized education and training, whether at the undergraduate level, graduate study, or advanced technical training.

At the Gannett Center in New York we conduct what we call "next generation" technology seminars for news executives, inviting newspaper, magazine, television, radio, and wire service people into the same sessions. If at first they are perplexed and uncomfortable in a seminar program with people from competing media, within minutes they clearly see mutual interests. Newspeople (in this case) are newspeople: They do many of the same things, and colleagues in other media may be well ahead or behind in terms of newsgathering techniques, text editing and graphics, management, audience research, or other aspects of news work. They learn a lot from one another and often begin to network outside their own medium as a result of such contact, something that is still nearly unheard of in the media industries, which so rarely talk to one another at the operational level.

Third, communication education must make better and more calibrated use of the university environment. It is important that communication educators not try to do the whole job of educating their students, that they skillfully draw on English departments, computer science, library science, and other fields. This means linking conceptual courses in communication in more intelligent ways with the general liberal arts curriculum. A journalism historian, for example, should not be teaching remedial U.S. history, a teacher of public affairs reporting ought not be a low-grade civics teacher layering material onto what ought to be the specialized domain of communication education. We need to better know and draw on the rest of the university to accomplish our own aims and objectives.

In recent years there has been great objection to suggestions that students possess a broad range of conceptual and craft needs not currently being provided by most schools of journalism and communication. The answer is not to overload an already top-heavy curriculum with more work in the major, but to make better use of what is already available in the university and to work collaboratively with others to better tailor courses to media students' needs if necessary. The seemingly helpless cry of the faculty member who feels trapped by curricular (and accreditation) constraints will be well-served by this approach.

Fourth, we need to take a greater leadership role in the university. Communication is central to society and ought to be central to universities and especially to students. A whole generation of media-illiterate students is emerging from American universities in the midst of a media society. A university graduate who has no concept of the role of communication in society, of freedom of expression, or how to use media to stay informed is not an educated person prepared for society today. It is incumbent upon communication educators to be advocates for communication literacy throughout the university. They should insist that courses providing a conceptual map of communication (or modules of courses in such fields as political science and sociology) be part of the university's core areas of knowledge.

Finally, educators need to look outside the groves of academe to industry to develop a strategy that allows them to better understand, interact with and influence the media and communications industries. It is no better to be ignorant and arrogant critics of the communications industry than it is to be slavish sycophants. Educators need a thoughtful strategy that allows them to better know and understand at a conceptual and operational level the media industries, both for themselves and their students. They also ought to be open to suggestions and ideas from the professional community while at the same time sharing research on questions that are important to industry. In the process, there is also room for criticism and analysis of the media. Most importantly, I believe, communication educators need to establish a dialogue of respect among people in the communications field, for their own benefit and that of their respective fields and society.

21. Looking Beyond Convergence[†]

If there is a single concept that marked the last decade, it is surely "convergence"—the coming together of communication devices and forms into a single electronically based, computer-driven mode that has been described as the nearly universal integration of systems that retrieve, process, and store text, data, sound, and image.

But convergence is much more than the stuff of hardware and software: It is the driving force that has spurred major change in the media industries and almost everywhere else. Although futurists long ago predicted a time when communication and computer technologies would converge and integrate, the connections to real life for many in the media industries seemed far away. But it quickly has become apparent that all forms of communication, all media, now have more commonalities than differences.

---

† *Communiqué* column, January 1990 (monthly newsletter of FFMSC).

This is true at the level of ownership and control, whether under a mostly commercial system like that of the United States or other quasi-governmental or state systems. Large enterprises now own print, broadcasting, cable, database, and other media industries, having organized them under a single corporate roof. And at the level of management, people are increasingly moving betwixt and between different media, something also evident and possible for other personnel as well.

Even the product has been touched by convergence. Who can say whether a national newspaper such as the *Wall Street Journal* or *USA TODAY* is a print or electronic medium? Both depend on satellites and computers to function.

Another aspect of convergence is the blurring of media functions—information, entertainment, opinion, and the advertising that surrounds and delivers them. In fact, it is now difficult to say what function is most responsible for the existence of a particular medium, except that most all have advertising.

There has long been a debate over the mixing of news and opinion, as in interpretative reporting, and the information-entertainment mix is at the heart of many recent controversies involving television, particularly the debate over "re-creations." In most instances, what is happening is heavily influenced by technological realities that survive when the marketplace responds and government removes regulatory roadblocks. Clearly, convergence has ushered in a united state of media, one that will continue to pose important and wrenching questions in the 1990s.

In the 1990s we will turn our attention increasingly to the consequences of convergence, for it will no longer be enough to simply understand it. There are economic, technological, and legal/regulatory dilemmas that will affect individuals and social institutions as well as society. These factors also ought to have great impact on the education and training of journalists and other communicators as some of the present medium-specific programs become increasingly isolated from and irrelevant to the real world.

Convergence is at the root of the growing globalism and giantism of our media organizations, which seem ever distant from any kind of human scale. At the same time it is convergence that has made possible the era of desktop publishing.

Amid this paradox between the macro scale of conglomerate media and those ultimately personal media and messages made possible by the personal computer, we need to understand, confront and ultimately connect with the consequences of convergence.

22. New News Technology: Death Knell or Challenge?[†]

In its formative decades, American television news was ever and always the beneficiary of new technology. It was, after all, technology's child, and even its infancy outdistanced and superseded radio. One technological triumph followed another. From a medium that was essentially a headline service of talking heads, it combined a special gift for immediacy with the filmmaker's art to create brilliant documentaries. And, as with the movies, black-and-white pictures soon gave way to color.

In the 1970s an era of electronic newsgathering made field reports easier and cheaper. Improvements in international transportation along with satellite transmission brought dramatic improvements in coverage. In one decade alone, videotape, which largely replaced film, radically changed both the immediacy and character of television news, especially international coverage.

Then, after an unbroken string of technological triumphs, television news was itself challenged by technologies that began to redefine the division of labor between national networks and local stations, between over-the-air broadcasting and cable. The once impenetrable strength of three national networks was severely tested in the 1980s, and many in television feared this medium might itself follow radio's course for decades ago when centralized command of national networks fell prey to localism and to a fragmentation that ended radio's reign as a medium with a national voice. This led some commentators to ask rhetorically, "Is television's future that of radio's past?" Will television news, long our witness to the modern world, play a less decisive, less important role in the next decade and beyond?

The reaction of television news as an institution to these great changes, especially at the network level, has been disappointing. For the medium that dethroned radio to respond Luddite fashion to change—rather than taking the high road and commanding that

---

† This chapter originally appeared January 1990 as an article in *Television Quarterly*, 251.

change—has been surprising. Arguably the smartest and most accomplished people in communications today have wallowed in self-pity, extolled the past, and denounced the future, which they see as a threat to their values. But is the change that economics and technology are bringing really antithetical to the very real accomplishments of the best of television news, either at the networks or at first-rate local news operations? A look at history suggests to me that pessimistic prospect need not be real.

Still, futurists in the 1990s are cautious as they look at television news, remembering the flawed forecasting of the 1970s when technological enthusiasts imagined a wired nation and a television of abundance. That abundance did come, but much later and in less diversity than predicted. The lesson worth remembering is that inventions and innovations, however impressive, must have both a market and a friendly regulatory climate.

Recall that commentators who predicted that every home would have 100-plus cable channels to select from by the 1980s—not to mention the benefits of interactivity, addressable messaging, high-fidelity sound, and higher-definition pictures, as well as teletext services in the home—were greatly disappointed. To be sure, the technology was there for commercial exploitation, but the market was not, nor were government regulators acting as cheerleaders for change.

Ironically, the futurists of that day never contemplated the economic impact of such new technologies as cable. It was as though they expected not only great population growth, but also a desire by consumers to almost infinitely increase their expenditures on information—and the advertising community to do so too.

Cable Competition

With the coming of cable alternatives ranging from CNN to ESPN, not to mention entertainment programming and recycled movies, the national networks, perhaps America's greatest contribution to contemporary popular culture, found themselves scrambling to hold audiences and the revenues that audiences would bring through advertising. Still preeminent in news, the national networks faced a challenge not only from Ted Turner's upstart Cable News Network, but from their own affiliates and other local stations.

Once considered as little more than a distribution system for the networks, plus adding their own parochial voice, local stations and station groups increasingly competed with networks for advertising and audience. They even ventured outside their own domain, going to the scene of breaking news almost anywhere on the globe, again threatening the once-exclusive franchise of the networks.

In the 1990s, it is still uncertain whether the networks and CNN will become the Associated Press of the future—that is, suppliers of programming and news content, or find a new niche that is clearly distinguished from the offerings of local stations, station groups, and other competitors. American network news companies, although the product of larger corporations, pale when compared with such global giants as Time Warner, Bertelsman, Hachette, and others poised on the commanding heights of an information economy. At the moment television news, like the great national newspapers of Europe, is essentially a national product: American fare largely for Americans. Whether that will change as the markets of Western Europe—not to mention the still sleeping giants of Central and Eastern Europe—seek more programming, cannot yet be determined.

Several factors could portend great growth for television news. The increasingly giant and global media marketplace will need the special offerings of television news. At the same time, once costly news programming can and should get cheaper. Newsgathering capabilities with smaller and lighter cameras as well as compact editing equipment are encouraging signs. So is the emergence of fiber optics, which will greatly enhance newsgathering, processing, and presentation.

Reconsider Interactive TV

Once abandoned as impractical and too costly, such technologies as interactive television and videotext services might be reconsidered. Though the Warner experiment with QUBE in Columbus, Ohio, in the 1970s may have failed, it has already reappeared in the form of televised consumer marketing services. Researchers and MIT's Media Lab have predicted the rise of personal newspapers, available electronically, and already the possibilities for pure information—such as lists, sports scores, and weather reports—are changing and challenging the traditional definition of news.

In the 1980s, television news continued to play with its techno-logical advances, not necessarily benefitting the viewer, but demon-strating certain capabilities with gusto. The first uses of electronic newsgathering (ENG) had more to do with demonstrating the tech-nologies than gathering the news. Cameras were set up to capture action and immediacy whether news was happening or not.

The networks demonstrated that they could go anywhere to broadcast, but often insisted that anchors be there on the ground to deliver the news. This tended to redefine news, not in terms of its actual importance, but in terms of where anchors could physically appear. While this captured great public attention, it had the effect of diminishing the value of genuine experts, such as foreign corre-spondents, whose work became the stuff of background reports. News by 1990 at the network level, as far as the public could tell, was defined as events that network anchors could describe from the site itself. This, of course, wasted the real advantages of technology that cut across time and space and which in fact did not need the physical presence of Tom Brokaw or Dan Rather on the ground at the Berlin Wall when they could have as easily discharged their duties from their desks in New York.

New Marvels in the Offing

At a time when the real innovations of recent decades have hardly been used to great advantage, even greater marvels of technology are in the offing. Communication and computer experts are, for example, experimenting with virtual reality, a three-dimensional world that allows the viewer to actually become a part of the picture. As one observer of this new world wrote, "Increasingly sophisticated programs simulate participation in 'real' worlds. Potential viewers can look at life through the eyes of a frog; take part in the French charge at Agincourt; chop off the head of an enemy; or become Warren Beatty in 'Shampoo.' "

Virtual reality is an ultimate form of interactive video wherein viewers can enjoy sensations not previously anticipated in the media. Still, it is doubtful that American television as now structured and organized will creatively cash in on such innovations.

Witness, for example, the disappointing performance of news simulations and recreations at the end of the 1980s. Used at first in show-off fashion and quite unethically, this exciting technology, which could give television news the vitality that dialogue and narration gave literary works, was abandoned because a few thoughtless users abused the technology. Henry Luce demonstrated the uses of dramatic re-creations in his "March of Time" series on radio and movies in the 1940s, but for some reason television news executives could not harness it effectively as an ethical enhancement to the news in the 1980s.

The reason for this and, I think, other disappointments of modern news programming, is the inability of news executives to experiment seriously with news programming and formats in an environment in which the threat of low ratings does not quash every innovation. The greatest energies at the present are concentrated on managing network news in a changing marketplace in which cable, local stations, and even VCR use are seen as the enemy. The networks scramble to present a distinctive product, making use of their vastly superior personnel, but often come up empty, presenting programs that are so much alike that viewers have trouble distinguishing one from another.

Creative Editing

As Sander Vanocur pointed out in a July 1990 speech in Prague, there is almost no attention to creative editing, to the internal processing of news that has always given a great news organization its distinctive character. The emphasis at the networks has been on gathering news, not on creative editing and presentation. Thus the form of television news, even with the wonders of ENG and computer graphics, advanced little in the late 1980s and early 1990s.

Indeed the main message of television news's most distinguished practitioners and commentators has been a celebration of the past, a veneration of the golden age of Edward R. Murrow, rather than a realistic assessment of the present economic climate with an eye on damage control and creativity. As major wrenching economic, technological, and regulatory changes have come to the networks in recent years, replete with wholesale firings and apparent cutbacks in news budgets, it has been understandably difficult for those who created a great system of network news to see any silver lining in the present disarray.

So an aging system of broadcasting—not electronic communication—marches on, making few changes in its format, clinging romantically to a past that seems more glorious with each passing month. Little is said about the real benefits of programs like "Nightline" or its imitators, the raw material feed of C-SPAN, or the ubiquitous presence of CNN. Jeff Greenfield and other thoughtful members of a new generation of network correspondents who certainly have not sold out to market forces, argue that the climate for news and public affairs is actually better today than in the past, but their views get few takers—at least not among pioneers of the golden age.

While network news readjusts to changing times, it has not often experimented with new formats and approaches. It may be in a position similar to that of newspapers in the 1970s when loss of circulation and declining advertising required great changes not only in formats and writing styles, but in the actual definition of news and in the organization of news staffs. Among the first signs of change for the print media was the controversial literary journalism of the new journalists. At first dismissed and despised, it eventually brought literary devices to the news and eventually helped liberate straightjacketed "objective" reporting. Newspaper editors, hardly agents of change, were pushed in part by market forces to save their enterprises by creating special sections, by covering news thematically instead of using conventional beats, by allowing for freer writing styles and courting new audiences.

Television news, especially at the network level, has not yet undergone such extensive reassessment. It may need to do so in order to survive in a world in which much essential information is available from other sources and where its one-time subalterns are now real competitors in their own right.

Always, of course, technology will offer tools for exploitation that will need to be harnessed and employed to proper purpose, perhaps on an experimental basis in local markets or at university television stations. The great contributions of the pioneers of television news from the 1950s forward set a standard for quality that need not be abandoned, but it must adjust to the realities of economics, technology, and regulation. The competitive environment is not only complicated by local and regional competitors but also by global forces.

The main lesson of the technology is that news can be gathered, edited, and distributed more cheaply than ever before, which is both a blessing and a curse, because networks do not automatically have a dominant position. What networks still have is a superior work force, made possible by two generations of dominance and the resultant prestige. Regulation, never kind to change but passive in the 1980s when deregulation lowered many barriers, might once again become a factor. Cable, in fact, will be the first of the communications industries to feel this influence, but because cable can no longer really be distinguished altogether from over-the-air broadcasting, anything affecting it will also be felt across the communications industry.

Experimentation Needed

More than anything, television news in the 1990s needs creativity and experimentation. It needs to know and understand its audience better, not relying mindlessly on conventional ratings, but engaging thoughtful analysts in a process of refined understanding of what will make the new audience of the year 2000. Television news, whether at a local or national level, needs to recognize and take advantage of the global economy, perhaps taking a lesson here from CNN, which is now piped into hotel rooms throughout the world and which also uses foreign product in its own productions.

As Adam Clayton Powell III, National Public Radio's former chief news executive, has written, "Changing technology may splinter the audience in ways that are now only dreams or nightmares, depending on your viewpoint. Perhaps the future of television news is not radio, after all: The future of television news may be magazines. Is CBS News to be *Collier's*? Or is it the AP of the future, feeding raw material to the new video vendors?" Or maybe something else, yet unimagined.

Logic suggests that a great system of newsgathering, processing, and dissemination will not have such a hard time adjusting to and leading the communications industry to the next form of news programming. But the next stages also rationally ought to be different if they are to remain preeminent and competitive with others who will challenge them in the next decade.

PART V

On Reportorial Imperatives

23. The First Hundred Days[†]

First impressions have a way of sticking. It is true for individuals and it is true for institutions. It may be especially true for the presidency, which is unique in that it is an institution whose character is shaped by the individual who occupies it.

The first impressions made by a new president—his personnel choices, his public remarks, and projected programs—are almost immediately codified into a public image. Ever since Franklin Roosevelt imposed a deadline on his new administration in its emergency measures to intervene in the Great Depression, the news media have been fond of measuring administrations in 100- or 1,000-day increments, using them to analyze the president's performance.

Because our news media value coverage of politics and government above all else in American life, the president truly sets the agenda for national news and, arguably, international news coverage. The chief executive, his cabinet officers, aides, and advisers, receive exhaustive coverage. Add to this press scrutiny of the president's personal life, and no other person or institution in the world today is the subject of so much media attention. What the White House cares about America cares about, and the items the president leaves off the agenda often get short shrift elsewhere.

This is not to say the press plays no role, of course. Walter Lippmann, hinted at the role the press plays in this agenda-setting business, but the idea first found full expression in the eloquent writings of political scientist Bernard Cohen, who explained that the media do not tell people what to think, but "what to think about." The scope of public discussion and debate is shaped by the symbiotic agenda-setting that begins in the White House with the president expressing himself on some issues and not on others, and is reified and reinforced by the press, which makes its own choices in determining what is newsworthy.

---

† *Communiqué* column, "The President's First Hundred Days," January 1989.

Presidents, like all leaders, like to control the information that comes out of the White House. They make Herculean efforts to see that their views and those of the administration get to the public. The press is instrumental in this process, of course, but it also performs a critical function, assessing the administration's performance, its goals and programs, and much more.

But critics say that presidential coverage has been immune to changing standards and styles of American journalism, which have otherwise greatly humanized coverage of public affairs.

Studies of White House coverage tend to confirm this. In recent decades there has been little truly imaginative or creative journalism coming from the White House press corps. Most stylistic innovations and new methods of reporting have been developed elsewhere. Some White House reporters respond by saying that their job is to cover fast-breaking daily events, that the place for reflection and analysis is "back in the office."

To be fair, White House reporters also enjoy little direct access to their subject. The much-ballyhooed presidential news conference suffers from great informational limitations, even at its best. Unlike many other democratic leaders, such as Britain's prime minister, our presidents are more insulated from meaningful access and critical comment, even when they hold frequent press conferences.

Still, we should cheer the work of scholars who often provide important new intelligence about the news conference. Attention should also be paid to new reportorial methods, especially computer-assisted reporting, that can enhance coverage of the paper-intensive business of government.

But perhaps somewhere in between there can be a role for the media in the day-to-day monitoring of the White House with regard to America's and the world's principal public problems. Is the president addressing them? If not, why not? Media people who can look broadly at topics vital to the nation's agenda, connecting them with public opinion and daily political reality, would do their fellow citizens a service in providing more critical coverage of the presidency.

24. When Race Becomes the News[†]

In the midst of racial turmoil and controversy in New York and other cities in the late 1980s, there have been predictions about a future filled with long, hot summers of rage and violence. Of course no one knows whether this will happen, but it has become something of a cliche since the late 1960s for the media to make such prognostications in the heat of racial and ethnic disputes.

Most of the time such speculation has been wrong. The idea that racial conflict is confined to the summer months is also something of a fallacy, born of the urban unrest of the 1960s, and particularly the violent summers of 1967 and 1968. Although there have been racially based conflicts and controversies throughout our history, no one is quite sure just when race becomes news. In 1988 and 1989 alone—when incidents such as those in Howard Beach, Bensonhurst, Central Park, Virginia Beach, and Boston were synonymous with violent acts, even murder, race was almost always there as one of the central issues, if not the pivotal cause of action that eventually became news. In the 1960s, when the Kerner Commission declared there were two Americas—one black and one white—many people resolved to create a more harmonious, multicultural society, one in which the media would play a larger, more conscientious role. It was clear then that we needed a media system that employed many more people from diverse racial and cultural backgrounds and that gave broader and more balanced coverage of minority communities. Those efforts have proceeded, slowly but with some result. Today there are national organizations of black, Hispanic, and Asian-American journalists, and though few media organizations have begun to reach the goals they set for themselves, many have made notable strides.

In the midst of these developments comes the steady flow of news in which race seems to be the determining factor in the newsworthiness of an event, issue, or trend. Too often the media define racial conflict in the most negative terms—in terms of crime, violence, epithets, demonstrations. At the same time we are well cautioned that race is not always a relevant factor in the news.

---

† *Communiqué* columns, "When Race Becomes the News," June 1990 and "Racial Diversity: An Essential If Elusive Goal," March 1991, monthly newsletter of FFMSC.

Almost every day somewhere in this country (not to mention the rest of the world) there are incidents and controversies incontrovertibly racial in character. But there are other human interactions in which the root cause is not essentially racial, although it is sometimes portrayed as such. On the one hand many news decision makers are careful not to ascribe too much importance to the race of an individual involved in, say, crimes related to drugs, while on the other hand some incidents of physical violence between, say, white police and black youths, might or might not have been ignited by racial factors.

Sometimes it really is difficult to determine whether race is relevant to the news. Years ago the use of racial labels in news stories, particularly negative ones, became suspect when people rightly asked whether such identification was pertinent. Now the formulation has become more complex, not only in the essentially negative news stories but in positive ones as well, sometimes in instances in which old barriers have been broken or a person is the first of his or her race to win an office or an honor.

Once we move beyond the anomaly stories, which can be quite paternalistic, the same rules that apply to other human interest portrayals ought to apply here. In 1954, when the Supreme Court decided *Brown v. Board of Education*, the landmark school desegregation case, there were hopes for a color-blind society in which factors other than race would be the determinants of news. In more recent years, this notion has been joined by a celebration of multicultural awareness in which race and ethnicity do indeed become a factor in the news, whether positive or negative.

Racial Diversity: An Essential if Elusive Goal

A spring 1991 visit to our center by Jesse Jackson and a seminar on racial diversity pointed up that minorities still have a long way to go in attaining a voice in the media. Moreover, the important goal of racial diversity in the newsroom may be in jeopardy.

Beginning with the civil rights movement in the 1950s and continuing through periods of considerable turmoil in the 1960s, the U.S. news media, which had for the most part ignored race as a factor in news, as well as in their own newsroom employment patterns, began to sing a different tune. Within a few years after the historic Kerner Commission Report there were minority recruitment efforts, special scholarship programs, endless conferences and expressions of support for a truly "inclusive" and "multicultural" media. Though there have been some signs of progress, the process has been painfully slow and only partly successful. True, there is more minority coverage today than was once the case and, true again, there is a more visible minority work force than was heretofore evident, but neither come anywhere near the media's own self-professed goals.

Especially slow has been the promotion of minority persons into positions of middle management and top leadership. The reasons for this situation are many, complex, and varied, but one problem seems to be a lack of genuine commitment tied to specific goals and objectives. The answer has not been found in setting quotas without offering a coherent program of recruitment, retention, and staff development or in exhorting the news media to engage in more extensive coverage without rigorous assessment of the quality and quantity of that coverage. In some instances, media organizations and various associations have spent more time diagnosing the problem and issuing excellent reports with depressing statistics than in prescribing treatment. Although piecemeal efforts, though well intentioned, can be helpful, what is needed is a broad-based communication industry effort to address the problem of representativeness by learning from each other and recognizing that in an age of convergence it is of limited value to view newspapers and television, for example, as separate and unrelated entities.

This is especially true in a recession, when newsroom layoffs, along with other cost-cutting measures, become more commonplace. In spite of this, organizations like the National Association of Black Journalists, the National Association of Hispanic Journalists, the Asian-American Journalists' Association, and the Native American Journalists Association have emerged as vigorous and important proponents of racial diversity in the media. They are astutely aware of the special peril that a recession presents. These groups are planning a first-ever joint national convention in 1994 in which to express their common bonds and mutual needs. Perhaps in concert with other groups of media professionals and industry organizations they can begin to look across and between the various elements of the communication industry. That can only happen when affected parties—and that is all of us—work together to harness industry, academic, and professional interest and muscle to do the job. Two projects developed at the Media Studies Center, for example—one by former fellow Dorothy Gilliam of the *Washington Post*, the other by staff—aimed at this objective. These projects were linked to previous efforts here and elsewhere, touching both on representative staffs and representative coverage in the media— great goals that deserve and demand more than lip service. The issue of racial diversity in the media is a dilemma tailor-made for scholarly and professional collaboration; the media could use the disciplined intelligence of research and assessment to help shape and monitor concrete plans and eventual accomplishments.

25. Mapping the Rape Victim Controversy[†]

As the undisciplined, emotionally charged controversy over naming the alleged rape victim in the Kennedy compound case unfolded in early May 1991, the media's inability to cover ambiguity and complexity became evident once again. While decisions by NBC and the *New York Times* to break with tradition ignited the controversy, nobody said much at all about the supermarket tabloid *Globe*, which was the first U.S. publication to name the alleged victim. These "wretched excess" papers engage in gossip usually too hot or scurrilous for the mainstream press to handle. Most of the time they are ignored by the major media more because of taste than accuracy.

Still, it was the *National Enquirer*'s photo of Gary Hart and Donna Rice that became one of the most lasting visual images of the 1988 presidential campaign. The public might rightly ask: When and under what circumstances do these outlaw papers set the agenda for the mainstream press? In much of the media discussion of the case, First Amendment press freedom, boldly interpreted, was pitted against the rights of privacy, especially the rights of persons involved in sex-related crimes. Less was said about the free press-fair trial

† *Communiqué* column, May 1991 (monthly newsletter of FFMSC).

implications of the coverage, which would have affected both the accused and the accuser in this case. Standards agreed to by much of the press after the 1963 assassination of President Kennedy (when Lee Harvey Oswald was called "the assassin," not the "alleged assassin") have largely been abandoned. At one time the voluntary rules written by the Reardon Commission of the American Bar Association were adopted across the country by free press-fair trial councils, widely distributed to reporters, and taught in journalism schools. The rules were based on the idea that people have some Sixth Amendment rights to a fair trial, protected from prejudicial publicity. In the Kennedy compound case the role of the press as an agent of change—promoting the worthy goal of destigmatizing victims of rape and other violent sex crimes—versus the reality of present-day attitudes and their impact on women caught up in such coverage was widely debated.

Here First Amendment absolutists were at odds with feminists, privacy advocates, and others. If the media had treated controversial news decisions in this case as they treat other public events, they might have mentioned the coincidental meeting of the American Society of Newspaper Editors held a few days before the NBC and *New York Times* decisions in which the issue was hotly debated. During that week, Alan Dershowitz, Harvard law professor, urged candor in the case and the *Des Moines Register* was honored with the Pulitzer Prize for a story about a rape victim who voluntarily went public in an effort to help destigmatize the victims of the crime. These facts, coupled with the longstanding absolutist First Amendment views of NBC President Michael Gartner, a former ASNE president, might have provided some basis for a better understanding of the decisions to print the name. The media might also have examined issues such as advertising and audience share at a time when network news was losing a large portion of its audience and each network jealously sought, as they do today, the greatest number of viewers. Not even the venerable *New York Times* is immune from marketplace pressure in a city where tabloid wars rage and a soft advertising market decreases profits.

The issue of whether to broadcast or publish a rape victim's name is complex, requiring more context and background than the press is willing to give it. In the end, it is clear once again that if the news media are to inspire the kind of public confidence essential to credibility in a democracy, a coherent and consistent set of standards for news decisions ought to be part of the public debate. The kinds of ethical inconsistencies that apply one standard to the Central Park jogger case, another to the *Des Moines Register* case, and yet another to the Kennedy compound case are no longer adequate. It may be time to reconvene another Reardon Commission to sort out this and other media-public disputes.

26. When Mental Health Makes News[†]

In the history of this country, the proper care and treatment of the mentally ill has often been ignored or accorded benign neglect more often than it has been given serious public attention. We can only speculate about what might have happened if President Franklin Pierce had written "yes" instead of "no" on legislation in 1848 that would have set aside revenues from the sale of public lands to benefit the indigent mentally ill. In spite of the impassioned pleas of the great reformer Dorothea Lynde Dix, President Pierce rejected the idea of public accountability for the mentally ill as "wards of the nation." Using a states' rights rationale, President Pierce defined the problem as one for states and municipalities and without subtlety diminished the importance of mental illness as a problem worthy of attention at the highest level of our government. More than a century passed before the White House again took up the plight of the mentally ill as a matter of national consideration. After important albeit brief attention during the 1960s in the administrations of John F. Kennedy and Lyndon B. Johnson, there was silence at 1600 Pennsylvania Avenue. Then during the 1970s there was again an all-too-brief beacon of hope and concern when then first lady Mrs. Rosalyn Carter took a special interest in the mentally ill, urging a more effective public and private partnership.

---

† Speech given and the Fourth Annual Rosalyn Carter Symposium on "Mental Health Policy, Mental Illness and the Media, the Next Step," titled "When Mental Health Makes News: Flashback and Flashforward," October 7, 1989, Carter Presidential Center, Atlanta, Georgia.

For better or worse, the news media in America, like Mr. Dooley's Supreme Court, "follow the election returns." In simple terms, this means that much of the media's agenda is set in Washington at the White House, as the values, public utterances and proposals of the president have enormous impact and influence on what the media report and write about.

Looking back in time, a documentarian might cut away to a series of vivid visual images that would illuminate the role and relationship of the media in portraying the plight of the mentally ill, in explaining complex problems of the human condition, and in sometimes exploiting them. We would see early reporters and book publishers talking with Dorothea Dix as she conducted her nationwide crusade that led to the creation of hospitals and services for the most acutely mentally ill. Next we would witness a young woman named Elizabeth Cochran, better known as "Nelly Bly," who as a reporter for Joseph Pulitzer's *New York World*, feigned insanity and got herself committed to the asylum on Blackwell's Island in New York City. Our visual journey would also reveal the front pages of her newspaper and others, which carried a prototypical expose, "Horrors of the Madhouse." We would encounter exposes again in press coverage of mental hospital conditions in such places as Chicago, Illinois; Topeka, Kansas; Milledgeville, Georgia; and Staten Island, New York. It was at Staten Island in 1972 and again in 1982 that Geraldo Rivera did for the Willowbrook State School for the Retarded what Ms. Cochran did for the New York Lunatic Asylum in 1887. We would also get fleeting glimpses of *Life* magazine's vivid photojournalism documenting asylum excesses in the 1940s as well as clips from memorable movies like *The Snakepit*. And as we approached the present day, there would be images from television drama linking mentally ill Vietnam veterans to violent crimes.

If the documentary were complete, we would be treated to quieter images of editors and mental health experts agreeing that terms like *lunatic, feeble-minded, crazy, fiend* and others were inappropriate in a compassionate society. There would also be news media revelations about links between homelessness and mental illness as well as the effect of mental hospital closings and funding deficiencies. If carefully done, our imaginary documentary would provide a comprehensive explanation of a relationship that is complex and convoluted, horrific and humanistic, caring and careless. It is a story of conflict and cooperation, hostility and reform.

William Allen White, in an introduction to Albert Deutsch's classic, *The Mentally Ill in America*, accurately stated that the conditions of the mentally ill in America over our history are "primarily attributable, not to the emotional and mental makeups of particular individuals, but to broad-based public attitudes corresponding closely to the general manners and mores and to society's phase of development at each stage of its evolution."

In those few words, Mr. White, who was one of the most respected newspaper editors in this century, also explicated the muddled portrayal of the mentally ill that has emanated from our news media from the days of the early republic to the present. The media are not very good at capturing the essence of public attitudes or social trends, which are the norm, and thus thought to be mundane. They are better at covering what they call "the news," and that usually involves individuals, institutions and interests that are somehow distinguishable from the norm or the mainstream. The press loves conflict and controversy far more than it does everyday activities and operations.

Put in terms of the mental health field and, specifically, the mentally ill, the press likes to see itself as a sentinel warning the public against danger. Thus, in that violence is sometimes associated with emotional impairment, it has not been uncommon for the press to carry stories about "escaped mental patients," presumably to alert the public to a potential danger. Of course, these stories are designed to capture television viewers and newspaper readers as well.

Over the years there have been thousands of negative stories about mentally ill persons, and while the nomenclature associated with them and their condition is now described in more humane language and with greater civility, the message is pretty much the same as it might have been in an era of screaming tabloid headlines.

Since the invention of the exposé, whether of mental hospital conditions, municipal corruption, or scandal in the White House, the media have come back again and again to this popular formula. CBS News' popular "Sixty Minutes" program has almost institutionalized the form. From the time of the muckrakers in the early 1900s, the expose has aimed at uncovering malfeasance in office, misappropriation of funds, and other scandals the public ought to be informed of and warned about. While the intent of journalists who do exposes is often honorable, the results sometimes are not. The effective expose can spur the removal of incompetent administrators and fuel the climate for legislation and increased appropriations for the mentally ill. Of course, an expose is by definition a shocking revelation, one that will not lend itself to continuity of coverage. In fact, most exposes have been followed by media neglect. A mental hospital that is poorly run and underfunded will get the spotlight of attention. There might be some public reaction and even some support, but, in time, interest flags and the out of sight, out of mind syndrome sets in again. It may be years before the hospital or program under scrutiny today gets attention again.

Ironically, some of the best intentions of both the press and the mental health movement have backfired. In an article I wrote with a psychiatrist some years ago, we traced what we called "the romance and rotomontade of community mental health," explaining that historically many solutions to mental health problems have been oversold, romanticized, and boasted about before they eventually failed and disappointed the public. This was true in the case of moral reform in the 1840s and with state mental hospitals in the 1930s, as well as with such specific treatment modalities as insulin therapy, electroconvulsive therapy, chemotherapy, and others. The media, eager to learn of a breakthrough, often create unrealistic expectations for treatment that will yield instant success. When this does not happen there is profound disappointment and, typically, public rejection. For a variety of reasons, the high hopes for the community mental health movement in the 1960s were dashed, even before funding cuts dismantled them, when mental health centers failed to solve the most acute problems of patients released from state mental hospitals.

Mental health has also traditionally made news when a prominent person's mental fitness is on the agenda, as with a presidential candidate. Witness the flurry of articles in 1988 about Michael Dukakis' rumored treatment for depression, which he and his doctors quickly denied. Sadly and perhaps understandably he did not use the occasion to commend psychiatric services to those who need them, but instead gave credence to the assumption underlying the press inquiry that any and all emotional problems cast great doubt on the future functioning or fitness of anyone who has ever had them. In 1972, revelations about Thomas Eagleton caused his removal from the Democratic national ticket, whether for reasons of mental illness per se or that gremlin so familiar in the 1988 election: character.

Mental illness and mental health programs also make news in quieter ways when social agencies initiate programs or when legislation makes its way through the federal or state governments. This coverage, which is often somewhat routine, is nonetheless part of the continuity of news media attention to the subject.

On occasion, people who have overcome emotional deficiencies or those who treat these problems have received favorable treatment in the media, thus rounding out a complex and rather fragmented pattern of interaction between the media and the mental health field. On the one hand, most of the major advances in the mental health field have eventually won the support of the media on their way to victories with the public, while at the same time an enlightened view of the most complex of fields is often blocked by recalcitrant and insensitive journalists. One doubts that Clifford Beers, author of *A Mind That Found Itself*, would have achieved a station in American life for the mental hygiene movement without media attention, most of it positive, or whether sympathetic and sensitive information about such topics as alcoholism, drug abuse, and suicide would have made an imprint on the public mind without the media.

What we have is not a failure to communicate, but two institutions, the media and the mental health field, with essentially different concerns but with many areas of mutual self-interest. For this mutual self-interest to be translated into press coverage that both serves the public and advances the cause of the mentally ill in America, there needs to be both better mutual understanding and respect.

First, the mental health field can be enormously helpful to the media by making sense of various problems associated with the human condition. Mental health professionals from various disciplines can assist the media in interpreting current social issues and human problems, not by simply promoting their own ends, but by taking part in a continuing conversation in the pages of the press on such consequential matters as human sexuality, childhood depression, school phobia, drug dependency, and others. Without engaging in instant diagnoses of particular individuals for the media, the mental health professions and voluntary groups can help explain human behavior, its strengths and failings.

Second, the mental health field can take a more active interest in learning how the media work, including the standards and practices of individual reporters, producers, and media organizations. This might also lead those in the mental health field to remove barriers that reporters face in trying to cover this sensitive field. Historically, mental health professionals have not been as open and forthcoming as they might be, and the resulting secrecy has often led to suspicion.

Third, the mental health field can capitalize on recent changes in the media that are moving away from event-oriented hard news toward process reporting, in which such topics as the future of the family, children's problems, and others are accorded a status once reserved only for visiting monarchs. This tendency, decried by some news critics, is actually a boon to humanistic communication. Though there is still a need for traditional reporting of public people and pronouncements, it may be that the most vital stories about the American people will be found in census data, attitude surveys, and other indicators of the human condition. Mental health professionals are uniquely qualified to discuss these considerations with knowledge and insight.

Fourth, rather than being a victim of media excesses and misunderstandings, the mental health field and those who advocate the cause of the mentally ill need to diagnose the problems of their current relationship with the media—local or national—and develop a strategy that improves it. If the present media depictions of the mentally ill are denigrating, misleading or out of context, the media ought to be told so, both in local newsrooms and through national media organizations. Some great advances in the language used to describe mentally ill persons came in the 1950s and 1960s in contacts between the American Society of Newspaper Editors and the American Psychiatric Association. This could be done again.

Fifth, just as the mental health field needs to know the media, so do media institutions need to inform themselves about mental illness, a serious problem with profound social consequences that affects millions of persons at some time in their lives. It is not enough to do hit-and-miss stories about the risk factors in mental illness or the potential danger presented by a psychotic person. Instead, there ought to be an active effort by the media to command the knowledge that has been generated by the mental health field. The exemplary programs aimed at training media people in mental health and behavioral science topics in the 1960s and 1970s ought to be reinstituted, whether with private foundation or federal support. We do not need scores of these programs, but a few are warranted. Similarly, journalism education programs that take up such topics as the environment, science, and economics might also direct their attention to the mentally ill, possibly in the context of the homeless as a first step.

Sixth, the leaders of the media industries need to recognize that there is great interest in the human condition, not cast simply in terms of acute mental illness or mental hospitals, but connected to the frailties of every life—the rage we all feel in a traffic jam or at a busy airport, the effect of hot weather on our behavior, the link between news of public affairs and individual attitudes and actions, and much more. Mental illness is something most Americans will experience either directly, in themselves or their own families, or indirectly, with friends and acquaintances. In an era when our media owners are said to have a monstrous vision guided by the values of Wall Street, covering mental health concerns is also good business. Mental health need not be a dreary story with images from *The Snakepit*. It also can be the story of preventive medicine and knowledge about mechanisms for coping with the most perplexing aspects of our angst-ridden modern life. Media people have much to gain—in public credibility and profits—by taking up this subject.

Finally, we need publicly expressed concern about mental health and mental illness at the highest level in this country—in government and politics and in business and other institutions. The press is largely a reactive institution. It will rarely initiate inquiries where there is little public dialogue and discourse, regardless of the importance of the topic. Thus, mental health leaders need to keep the pressure on leaders in all of the great institutions of American life from those basic building blocks—the family, the church, and the school—to others like business, government, labor, and education.

How people cope with the 1990s is a story of great importance, whether cast in terms of economics, politics, technology, or social issues. The media and mental health fields both have a stake in fostering better public understanding of how and why people function the way they do. They ought to find ways to work cooperatively toward this end.

27. The Whole World Watches—Again[†]

Walter Cronkite, John Chancellor, and David Brinkley—three deans of broadcast journalism—were once asked about the greatest story of their career. Without flinching, each answered, "World War II, of course."

There is something about war and the threat of war that quickens the journalistic pulse. In a humanitarian sense journalists abhor the destruction and casualties that come with any armed conflict, but at the same time war is the ultimate news story, with every element of newsworthiness.

War and the threat of war are all-consuming topics for the media, pushing other important stories—for example a Supreme Court nominee—off the front pages and the evening newscasts. This also points up the problematic nature of news. In the late 1980s Iraq was hardly noticed and Saddam Hussein received only scant attention in media surveillance of world leaders. In 1990, that all changed.

There was a tendency for the story of the Persian Gulf crisis to follow two tracks—one of grand and global politics with bellicose charges between and among governments, and another of right and wrong, of hero and villain. Sometimes what is essentially an economic story, a story about the world's oil supply, the main motivation for all involved parties, gets buried. While the whole world watches, the media try to map out the territory, to explain who the parties are and what they are saying, to assay interests and motivations. And they go beyond the story of global politics to the people on the ground, the military personnel who ultimately fight a war if there is to be one. But sometimes this coverage, while well intentioned, trivializes the larger issues.

The press's track record in previous conflicts is not exemplary. As Phillip Knightley wrote in *The First Casualty*, arguably the best book written on war correspondence, most war coverage is little more than cheerleading. Principles of balance and fairness, supposedly the cornerstones of faith for the Western media, often yield to coverage that is supportive, patriotic, and sometimes even jingoistic. Exceptions to this are few and far between.

---

† *Communiqué* column, September 1990 (monthly newsletter of FFMSC).

The Persian Gulf crisis may have been the first great test for the media in a modern information society and a global economy. Whether we and our counterparts in the world will be capable of reporting with a worldly, as opposed to a nationalistic perspective, will be an important indicator of the media's evolution. Undoubtably there will be a strong tendency for reporting to follow the traditional simplistic lines, to personify the conflict, and to emphasize troop movements over the complex economic realities.

Never before have we had the immediacy of modern communication in anything as complicated as the crisis in the Saudi desert. "Media diplomacy" is moving rapidly ahead of the normal diplomatic channels. Leaders on both sides make appeals to their citizenry through direct television exposure. We may not yet have the tools to cope with this very different kind of post-Cold War conflict, especially when the subtleties are channeled through technological wonders that were not heretofore a part of the media and military landscape. In the end it is the mission of the media to keep their audiences informed by surveying the international drama of this and other events. The present challenge is a profoundly difficult one that requires first-rate information for an active, analytical, and possibly even critical audience.

28. Communications and the Art World[†]

At first glance the art world and the media seem to occupy different regions of experience, their direct connections few and perfunctory. After all, the arts are rarely the stuff of riveting news stories, nor do they seem to have much in common with the mass media. It is the difference between the highest form of human expression and the utilitarian world of public communication, between high culture and popular culture.

But this is not really so. Both the media and the arts are engaged in and reliant on freedom of expression. They represent different

---

† *Communiqué* column, April 1990 (monthly newsletter of FFMSC).

branches of the same family, and they have continuous and important conversations with each other.

If once such fine arts as painting, music, and dance seemed to operate in their own world, this is no more. The arts need exposure and understanding if they are to survive and prosper in a market economy, and in all their forms they benefit from assessment, analysis, and criticism. The arts must have more than diplomatic relations with the information, entertainment, and opinion media.

By the same token, the rights of a free press are in some measure dependent on the press's encouragement and support of artistic freedom. In 1990, controversies involving public funding of controversial exhibits, such as Robert Mapplethorpe's photographs or Andres Serrano's paintings, again focused attention on the relationship between the arts and public opinion.

On another level, the media cannot be fully in touch with their audiences unless they know and appreciate the arts. Coverage and criticism of the arts are increasingly staples of print and electronic media, and our entertainment media rely on fiction, music, dance, and other arts for their substantive "content." Opinion journals and editorialists regularly comment on and try to encourage (or discourage) arts and artists in a fashion that, in Harold Lasswell's words, transmits the social heritage from one generation to another. And, increasingly, advertising media and advertising messages draw upon, promote, and encourage the arts.

The arts in every society have had their patrons—nobles, tycoons, foundations, government, and others. Today the media are the most important link between the arts and the various publics they appeal to or serve. Both benefit from each other's company, though the record of media treatment of the arts is mixed at best.

Arts coverage, while on the rise, is largely superficial, and some of the arts rarely get recognition or coverage. Sometimes criticism in the media is uninformed, more harmful than helpful, and almost every field of the arts complains regularly about not getting fair publicity, or even its fair share of publicity.

The media and the arts community do not always agree on what is important either. Often the media are drawn to celebrity and in the process celebrate an Andy Warhol while ignoring a whole school of modern artists who might also deserve notice. Prince Charles' critique of modern architecture gets more attention than a legion of architects and architectural critics who have devoted their lives to what they term *environmental art*. And on it goes.

On the media side, those who control communication enterprises sometimes find arts uncooperative, even hostile and self-serving. Some arts people are skilled at public relations while others are not. Many do not live very comfortably in the modern media world. But in spite of the tensions that exist, people in the arts and people in the media realize that it is advantageous to them both to find common ground on the plain of public opinion where they can foster awareness and appreciation for their respective worlds of expression.

Jane Addams, who founded Chicago's Hull House in 1889, used to say that the human spirit needed to be fed and housed but could not truly soar without art and culture. She might have added freedom of communication to her equation because today, when the media and the arts do more than merely coexist, they benefit all of us enormously.

PART VI

On Industry Connections

29. A Prescription for Economic Health[†]

As the largest component of the communications industry, newspaper publishing in the 1990s wants to hold and extend its economic and social impact. Contrary to popular predictions, the newspaper industry's preeminence in ad revenues, paid subscribers, and number of employees was not overtaken by electronic media in the 1980s, and no one seriously thinks this will happen in the new decade.

This is not to say that newspaper publishing has gone unchallenged. The electronic media have larger audiences and are demonstrably regarded as the most important source of immediate news for most Americans, but that has not yet translated into economic ascendancy for television, cable TV, or various new technologies.

This may be because newspapers individually, in groups and as an industry have engaged in what might be termed *creative damage control* for nearly two decades. With greater marketing sophistication, a repackaged "product" and a variety of new reader services, the newspaper whose role was being severely challenged in the 1970s recovered sufficiently in the 1980s to be regarded once again as modern and highly competitive.

Although newspapers have coped with change by increasing their reach in the morning and on Sunday, the 1990s may be a seminal time to consider anew the forces that would dethrone them from their commanding perch in the communications industry.

In the 1980s newspapers successfully navigated around economic challenges from other media, the accelerating pace of new technologies, and regulatory and legal threats.

These same forces are again poised to challenge newspaper ascendancy, although the challenge at first may happen incrementally—in tiny transactions that will not seem to warrant much consideration.

Economic challenges. The greatest economic challenge remains the electronic media, perhaps cable in particular because of its new and

† This chapter originally appeared August 1991 in the *Newspaper Financial Executive Journal*, pp. 3-5.

growing reach (now 53% of households) and extensive diversification of programming. Recall that the 1980s began with most viewers having only five or six channel choices, and compare that with the abundance of 1990.

Cable, which once relied exclusively on user fees for revenue, has made important strides in increasing local and national advertising revenues. This makes traditional broadcasters—local stations and networks—even more feverishly competitive. Similarly, magazines trumpet their ability to reach targeted, specialized audiences.

For all media, the problem is sharing a growing but finite amount of advertising revenue. Too many media competitors seek too little potential revenue, whether from advertisers or subscribers.

Newspapers naturally want to hold their place in the revenue pecking order and happily point to increases in the population segment—persons over 40—most likely to read newspapers. Other media, however, are eyeing the same potential customers.

Technological threats. No one can predict with certainty whether the 1990s will see a rerun of newspapers' videotext and teletext experiments, much additional work on fax newspapers, or heavy newspaper involvement in the lucrative business information and electronic database field. It is clear, however, that newspaper industry leaders, conscious of technological tools and challenges, must exploit market opportunities when they arise.

Industry leaders must also keep an eye on cable, personal computers, and videocassette recorder penetration if they are to evaluate properly the newspaper delivery system. Obviously, the Constitution does not require hard copy or delivery by truck or bicycle.

For those with a long memory, the modest development of facsimile newspapers in the 1980s underscores the fact that we should never discount a "new" technology. In the 1930s and 1940s, about 20 newspapers experimented with fax delivery, only to abandon it for lack of an appreciative market willing to pay the freight. Fax returned in the 1980s as an important technology—not yet for newspapers—aiming more at business than home use.

This raises questions about what other abandoned technologies might reappear, as well as what distinctly new ones might emerge.

Television promises great viewer and production advantages with high-definition television, while the dormant dream of interactive media has come to life in the form of home shopping services and electronic mail. Wise newspaper executives will stay tuned and ahead of the curve in this evolving technological saga.

Law and regulations. Although American newspapers are rightly proud of their distance from regulatory forces, it was government that kept the wolf from their door in the debate over electronic Yellow Pages.

As the regional Bell operating companies clamor to be released from the constraints applied under terms of the divestiture of AT&T, the phone companies are poised to deliver consumer classifieds and other kinds of information. The threat to newspaper classified advertising is obvious.

The communications industry abounds with other regulatory legal battles among various media. Whether this takes the form of cross-ownership rules, telephone-cable disputes, or content regulation, newspapers will be alert to push in the 1990s to extend to electronic media the same rights newspapers have.

Because it is increasingly difficult to technically define and distinguish print from electronic media, as newspapers use satellite transmissions and store text electronically, the arguments raised in the 1990s may get more converts than in the past. The convergence of all forms of communication into a single electronically based, computer-driven mode already has profound implications for newspapers and other media, but it remains largely undefined. This may be because the United States is among the last industrialized nations without a modern communications policy.

In an era of giant media companies and global competition, the idea of some mechanism for coherent policy will surely revisit us. The legal/regulatory framework we fashion in the 1990s will govern ownership at a time when new, nonpublishing interests—some of them international—will demonstrate eagerness to acquire more American newspapers and other media.

Navigating the economic, technological, and regulatory forces that themselves converge one into the other is a complex task that requires much more coherent planning than the newspaper industry has previously welcomed. Although scores of voices contribute to the pluralistic policymaking decisions that affect newspapers' future, newspapers themselves have not been big spenders on research and development.

What newspapers do best. At the root, communications media have only three functions: information, opinion, and entertainment. They also market goods and services through advertising but only as a sales agent for content.

Newspapers long ago lost the entertainment battle. Although they continue to entertain marginally with comic strips, puzzles, contests, and other features, no one seriously thinks newspapers challenge the preeminence of other media—especially television—as entertainers.

The newspaper's information function is its greatest strength—the main stimulus for audience and advertising interest. But the paper's role as information provider is also under assault by electronic media and databases. Such competition should be monitored carefully to see what value added elements newspapers can offer.

Newspapers deliver two commodities that electronic databases do not: well-edited, coherent news reports and, even more vital, opinions in editorials, columns, or op-ed pages. It was, after all, the free exchange of opinion even more than news that got the press special protection under the First Amendment. Newspapers do not do much to promote opinion sections, yet these pages may be their most important and distinguishable asset.

The future. How should newspapers react to competitive forces in the communications industry in the 1990s? In two ways, I think:

- *Newspapers should restate in subtle yet overt ways their information and opinion role.* This should be showcased, celebrated, and promoted as the essential core of our communications system—a source of disciplined intelligence for the public. At the same time, newspaper people from top leadership to entry-level personnel must engage in continuing conversation about content and format changes. Members of the public should also be solicited for their views about press performance.
- *Newspapers sit on the largest and richest databases in their communities without fully exploiting them.* In the 1980s business information services and specialized newsletters became big business, generating revenues nearly one-fourth as large as the whole newspaper industry. Many of these once little businesses were begun on personal computers in basements by persons obtaining information from public sources. With some imagination, newspapers should explore new revenue streams to be tapped by packaging information already gathered. Newspapers ought to encourage creative joint ventures with other media, their own employees, or other businesses, recycling information that may not belong in a general-circulation daily but that could have a place in a specialized newsletter or data service. A few, of course, are already doing this.

The 1990s will be a crucial time for newspapers to reaffirm their role in democracy by asking whether they are fully and responsibly covering their communities, making themselves accessible economically and intellectually to all potential readers, and defining *the public interest* as it manifests itself in international, national, and local issues and controversies.

In the midst of industry meetings, market research, and talk of "products" and "positioning," newspapers just might want to reflect on their uniqueness as an instrument of communication in a democracy in which intelligent decision making and economic survival depend more and more on accurate, competent and complete information.

30. The Newspaper: Alive and Well at 300[†]

In the summer of 1990, the only extant copy of the first issue of *Publick Occurrences Both Forreign and Domestick*, America's first daily newspaper, made a journey across the Atlantic from the Public Records Office in London where it regularly resides. It came to America to join a Library of Congress exhibition called "The American Journalist: Paradox of the Press," which had its origins in Loren Ghiglione's fellowship project at the Gannett Center.

Although this singular copy is the only trace of a publication that inaugurated newspaper publishing in America, the tradition it started is still very much alive in America today. In the three centuries since 1690, newspapers in America have gone through several life cycles.

Once available only to the elite, by the 1830s newspapers were accessible to common people, and by the 1890s they had become a mass medium. Along the way new media have evolved and have at times preempted some of the newspaper's former functions. Originally established to provide a flow of information and opinion, in time newspapers also brought their readers entertainment such as serialized

---

† *Communiqué* column, November 1990 (monthly newsletter of FFMSC).

novels, comic strips, and sports. Eventually radio and television commanded immediate news and killed the "scoop" and the "extra," two conventions of newspapers in the days when street sales were predominant. Television and magazines took over entertainment and again altered the function of the newspaper.

Currently there is much discussion about the future of the newspaper. Years ago Marshall McLuhan tried to write an obituary for newspapers, but the broadsheets refused to die. Instead their owners discovered market segmentation and fiercely staged a comeback in the 1970s and 1980s, both in circulation and market penetration.

In more recent years, as newspaper profits—still quite high by any comparative industry standard—have declined and advertising revenues have leveled off, analysts are again asking questions about the health of the newspaper industry.

Most indicators suggest that newspapers will continue to define their niche in the media family. They still account for a disproportionately large share of advertising expenditures in the United States, and they still have a vitally important role as sense-makers and interpreters of public affairs and public life. Moreover, newspapers are agenda-setters. They play a major role in determining what is news and influence not only other media, but all kinds of people from high-profile leaders to average citizens.

But newspapers are not without their troubles. Their owners are worried about declining profits, a soft advertising market and a fickle readership. Industry critics decry a lack of strategic planning and a scarcity of inspired leaders. They are also concerned about the decreasing number of truly exciting, well-managed newspapers in the country, whether independently owned or owned by groups.

To be sure, some characteristics of newspapers are quite anachronistic: paper products in an age of electronic impulses; serious-minded digests of news in an age of entertainment; and cranky critics in an age of consensus.

But don't be fooled by appearances. These enterprises are also heavy users of electronic communication, relying on computers for their internal functions as well as the gathering and dissemination of news and information.

Newspapers are leaders in ethics and professionalism compared with other media, and they are still the conscience among their information-industry counterparts. They have also been the most enthusiastic supporters of education and training for journalists.

There is not much similarity between *Publick Occurrences* and the typical newspaper today, but what a testimonial that this medium has survived so well and so long. Amid handwringing, it is also worth celebrating the 300th birthday of the newspaper and its great imprint on our life and culture.

31. TV at 50: All Its Glitter Is Not Gold[†]

In the seasons of an institution's life, age 50 is not exactly long in the tooth. But it is old enough to have achieved a certain maturity. In the many tributes to television on its recent 50th birthday, we celebrate the extraordinary achievements of a medium that has truly captivated the nation.

It is not hard to chart with appreciation and pride the evolution and development of news and public affairs programming, entertainment, sports, and even television advertising. As critics are wont to say, the body of work is breathtaking, the lifetime achievement extraordinary.

But what of quality? From black-and-white pictures to color and now on to high definition television, not to mention the magic of satellite transmissions and the hopes for interactive video, the accelerated technical maturity of television is incontrovertible. But successful television takes many forms. There is technical success and, most importantly, economic success for a medium that has become the world's preeminent communicator, far outdistancing print, radio, and others.

But when we ask whether the medium has really matured, the question of quality programming is preeminent. Here our 50-year-old friend becomes less attractive, for the medium that has done such distinguished work tends increasingly toward sensationalism.

For most of its history broadcast television had little competition and consequently its profits spiraled ever upward. The grip of the networks and their local affiliates loosened a bit with the coming of new media, especially cable and video cassette recorders, and while

---

† *Communiqué* column, May 1989 (monthly newsletter of FFMSC).

the networks are still preeminent and powerful, they must now compete with these new services in order to retain a strong audience share and advertising support. In the short run the great fight for prime-time supremacy seems to be a calculated assault on quality television programming. First-rate dramatic and public affairs programming have been affected by the rise of so-called "trash television," shows that bring the sensibility of the *National Enquirer* to the airwaves.

Along with mindless game shows and tasteless intrusions on privacy, a good deal of today's programming has abandoned standards and quality control in favor of quick profits. Few think that these outrageous shows will have great staying power, but they are capable of pushing up ratings over the short run and outdistancing less sensational programming.

The latest chapter of this downward slide is yet another example of sensationalist fare: "crash TV," a rude mixture of the elements of all-star wrestling, MTV, and various game shows. One such show, "Roller Games," gained broadcast commitments from TV stations covering 80% of the nation's viewing audience. The show features teams of skaters in scanty costumes leaping over snakepits and dodging laser beams while ambulances sit nearby to pick up the human carnage.

This and other crash TV offerings (with names like "Interceptor" and "American Gladiator") showcase athletes in outrageous costumes emulating thugs, pro wrestlers or prostitutes, adding another chapter to the downward direction of entertainment fare on television.

Part of the problem is genuine confusion about whether television can survive as a mass medium—one that really does command millions of viewers, all riveted to a single program—or whether it will become increasingly segmented, reaching discrete audiences and markets in the fashion of magazines. The prevailing assumption is that some mass television will survive but that there will also be segmented and targeted services with more limited numbers of viewers.

As this battle for viewers and advertiser support heats up, we may see a frenetic transformation of television. Perhaps in the end, for the same reason that newspapers like the *New York Times* do not court the same readership as the supermarket tabloids, television will really come of age and take a chance by doing what in the end will serve the American people.

Thus we ought to observe this half-century of television with caution, saluting the many contributions to human understanding that are gifts from entertainment and informational programming—some of it including creative games and sports, as well as absurd comedies.

At the same time, viewers ought to demand better fare than they are now getting. There is a long track record of commercially successful, quality programming, and there is hope that the impulses that created it will outlive the hit-and-run pandering that seems to be in vogue.

32. When the Regents Said "No"[†]

> *The insidious destruction of the lives and values of kids that those two minutes a day (of advertising) can accomplish means to me that we've got to say here: "Absolutely no. At least for the time that those kids are under our care you will not do this."*
>
> Shirley C. Brown, New York State Board of Regents

The Regents of New York State were unequivocal when they voted unanimously in 1989 to bar Chris Whittle's 12-minute news programs from the state's public schools. The schools, they said, should be a protected zone, free from the intrusions of slickly packaged programs and commercials on Whittle's Channel One.

The notion that schools at all levels should distance themselves from the reality and values of crass commercialism is an old and honorable tradition. Still, the regents' action and similar discussions elsewhere in the country are a departure from accepted practices. Schools have never been free from commercialism and there is even some reason to doubt that they should be. The same school boards that bar the Whittle Communications programming accept computers from IBM, Apple, and other vendors who presumably want their wares in the schools so that students will become devoted future users.

---

† *Communiqué* column, July/August 1989 (monthly newsletter of FFMSC).

Likewise, newspapers—many of which are hostile to the Channel One venture—participate eagerly in a "Newspaper in the Classroom" program, the goal of which, of course, is to give students the newspaper habit, to make them not only regular readers but also consumers of the products newspapers advertise. No newspaper or magazine I know of ever produced an advertising-free product for the schools.

Even the venerable *My Weekly Reader*, though not an advertising medium per se, worked its way into schools in which commercial products such as Crayolas and LePage's glue were readily accepted and used. Book publishers have never tried to hide their professional identity as they turn a handsome profit on textbooks and other materials, and yearbook companies, virtual institutions in American schools, sell everything from photographs to class rings. Schools themselves engage in commercial activity, engaging in fundraising activities by turning their student charges into sales forces hawking magazines, candy bars, and other products.

Thus the world that Chris Whittle asks to enter is hardly unsullied by commercial culture. Stopping him in the New York public schools, which may be a perfectly defensible position, will not undo an essentially commercial environment in which children and adults navigate betwixt and between a barrage of advertising. Just why the regents barred Channel One may have little to do with their general attitudes about a commercially driven capitalist society. But it does suggest the need for a much more persuasive and coherent policy about exposing children to the economic marketplace.

The policy in New York State and elsewhere in the nation allows students to use equipment emblazoned with the trademark of a computer firm but not to watch television programs sponsored by athletic shoe companies. Perhaps one form of advertisement is more subtle than the other, but both seek similar ends.

It also seems strange that there should be such consternation over commercialism at a time when commercial speech is winning court battles and establishing just as firm a footing on the American scene as political speech.

Far better, it seems to me, is to find intelligible ways to make young people discerning and intelligent consumers rather than pretend that commercialism does not exist. The bombardment we get from television, print media, outdoor advertising, and other forms of honorable paid advertising can hardly be ignored. Moreover, whether the schools can realistically reverse themselves and become a protected zone is highly debatable.

Another bothersome aspect of the regents' case is the kind of prior restraint it represents, a form of censorship in which a communications channel is closed by administrative fiat without consideration or consent from the potential consumers, their teachers, or parents.

Perhaps the regents need to look more closely at their overall standard, if indeed there is one. Clearly it is good public policy to bar the village pornographer, the drug dealer, cigarette and liquor vendors, and other obvious threats to public welfare. But without an enunciated public policy, the Whittle decision stands in isolation and the regents are left with case-by-case determinations in the future.

The regents' decision in the Whittle case may have the impact, however, of deterring other vendors who would like to make inroads with the youth audience courtesy of the schools. Had Whittle been competing against programming produced, say, by CBS or MacNeil-Lehrer (one with commercials, the other with grant money acknowledgement), it would have provided a better test for the underlying concerns in this important discussion.

33. The Search for Institutional Memory[†]

Complaints that the media have no institutional memory are frequently made by people upset about shortcomings of media performance, whether they involve marketplace transactions by media owners, the salaries of network superstars, or even more generally, the relationships between reporters and their sources.

All of these issues and more have been in the news recently and not surprisingly they have been treated with breathless wonderment, usually without background or context.

A modest attempt to correct part of that problem began in 1990 when the American Society of Newspaper Editors' Task Force on the History of Newspapers met at the Gannett Center. With several

---

† *Communiqué* column, April 1989 (monthly newsletter of FFMSC).

leading editors and journalism historians as members, the group hopes to encourage newspapers to preserve not only actual copies of their newspapers (something not universally done these days) but also correspondence, business records, and other materials that will be of value to historians, the press, and presumably the public.

It is a fine start for one branch of the media industries. It will not solve immediately, however, the problem of myopic media coverage of the media, which seems to be done with little reference to the substantial literature of communication history, ethics, economics, and theory.

In recent days such context and connection would have been a wonderful service to the public, which faces the most primitive kind of coverage of several arresting issues. For example: articles by Janet Malcolm in *The New Yorker* involving the propriety and appropriateness of the source-writer relationship between Joe McGinniss and Dr. Jeffrey McDonald, both of *Fatal Attraction* fame.

The underlying issues that truly became the "talk of the town" never even hinted that this is an age-old topic, one that is addressed specifically in at least 10 new books on media ethics, some of them even available in New York bookstores. Even McGinniss's own specific operational style was the subject of much discussion in the 1970s when a series of articles he did on Senator George McGovern were compared with his earlier writings in *The Selling of the President*.

All this was as lost as ancient Egyptian artifacts in the current debate. Another issue—the escalation of network salaries set off by Diane Sawyer's and Connie Chung's network hopping—did get cross-referenced to Barbara Walters' million dollar deal a decade ago, but that was about all.

Did scolding press critics know about the wholesale buying and selling of entire newspaper staffs in the era of Pulitzer and Hearst? Were the factors that made editor Arthur Brisbane the highest paid journalist of his day not the same ones at work in Connie Chung's negotiations?

Issues of public disclosure and institutional loyalty have been debated for a long time, but who would have known it from the textureless coverage of these developments? They and the recent Time-Warner merger would have benefitted from some sense of history, as well as acquaintance with the burgeoning literature of media economics.

Understanding of and appreciation for the Time-Warner deal also benefits from knowledge of communication theory. From the

Shannon and Weaver model of the 1940s to elegantly simple formulations that explain the process and effects of communication, one gleans a sense of how communication occurs in the abstract, free from specific technologies and individual media. The transmission and receipt of messages, the feedback function and much more help to sort out what is happening in the modern world of communication in which, increasingly, a single electronically based, computer-driven system is at the root of all communication, whether electronic or print.

All this argues for a more systematic connection between formal media studies and the media industries, presuming that media people have some incentive to know about the field of which they are a part. Even if they do not, however, the interested public ought to have access to better information.

We would not cover politics without a sense of history and we should do no less in our coverage of media. Increasingly, knowing one's field has to extend beyond personal experience, because few media people are widely acquainted with more than one medium and are rarely steeped in the history, economics, or ethics of their own field.

The ASNE task force may be the beginning of a number of joint ventures between industry and the academy that will help the media build its institutional memory and more intelligently assess itself.

PART VII

On the Media at War

34. The Gulf Crisis: Learning to Cover War Again[†]

Shortly after the Iraqi invasion of Kuwait on August 2, 1990, the idea that the United States might go to war seemed both fanciful and unlikely. After all, except for brief interventions in Libya, Grenada, and Panama, the United States had not been to war since Vietnam, which for many people was a memory that films like *Platoon* and *Born on the Fourth of July* have chronicled.

The news media dutifully and competently covered Saddam Hussein's forces as they drove the Kuwaiti government out of Kuwait City and took over what was typically given the clichéd descriptor, "tiny oil-rich kingdom." Almost at once, a multifaceted news strategy ensued involving coverage of action on the ground in the Gulf, activities in several interested and affected capitals, and diplomatic initiatives and determinations at the United Nations. The "story" had governmental and economic implications and was seen essentially as a distant artifact of public policy until American naval aid and ground forces began to move with greater numbers into the region in early fall.

By the time congressional debates were in full flower in November, media coverage was echoing the language of war drawn from the speeches of legislators, diplomats, and governmental officials here and elsewhere. Press coverage then became essentially debate coverage—presenting the points of view expressed in the House and Senate as President Bush got permission to proceed with what would become active warfare on January 16, 1991.

The Pentagon Versus the Press

While the administration was developing a strategy of support for its policy through briefings and press conferences, there was in

---

[†] This chapter was originally published March/April 1991 as an article in *The Public Perspective*: "The Media and the Persian Gulf: Learning to Cover War Again."

the Pentagon growing sentiment that "never again" would the media be allowed to undermine the war effort as the generals believed it had in the Vietnam conflict. Rules for coverage were promulgated and presented in late autumn. After the press denounced their restrictive and, some said, Draconian nature, they were modified, but the revisions still met media disapproval. Nevertheless the rules, aimed at preventing the release of information that would interfere with military operations or endanger the lives of troops, were set forth.

Amid questions about "whose side are you on anyway?" the news media, especially the major broadcast and cable networks as well as nationally oriented newspapers, had to consider practically how (and with what approach) they would cover the war should one ensue. Though media people argue that they are engaged in impartial and objective observation and reporting, they are, in fact, part of a communication system that is essentially national (and sometimes nationalistic) in character and operation. The U.S. media in wartime essentially report on and cover the war with U.S. news sources from an American viewpoint for an American audience.

Vietnam as the Exception

Contemporary reporters who had not previously covered war, and journalists with little institutional memory, did not know, for example, that throughout history reporters have most often been supportive of their side in any war, as Philip Knightly's (1976) book *The First Casualty* amply documents. For most wars in our experience, except Vietnam, war correspondents traveled with the troops and were assigned to units. Some even wore uniforms. Our images of great war correspondents—from Richard Harding Davis to Edward R. Murrow, and Ernie Pyle—were of chroniclers of war clearly sympathetic to our side.

Censorship—except in Vietnam—has been commonplace in all wars and especially in recent years in Grenada, Panama, and in the British-Argentine conflict in the Falkland Islands. Although Vietnam was different both in the freedom given to correspondents and in some of their reports that were highly critical, even in that war many correspondents were more cheerleaders than critics.

Journalists' Education

But the media in covering the events leading up to the Persian Gulf War as well as the six-week war itself, had little time to be concerned about history. Although they cited the Vietnam War, for the most part they knew little about it. Although they are fond of painting a picture of a rigorous, investigative press corps in Vietnam—and though their critics accept much of this interpretation of the press's performance, in faulting it for undermining the war effort—the picture of a "critical," investigative press in Vietnam is wildly exaggerated. It is true that late in that war television coverage of military action brought to us conflicting and critical information that was sometimes linked to declining confidence in and eventual public opposition to the war—though survey data show a more complex picture of the public's views and response. Memorable performances by the press in Vietnam, like those by David Halberstam, were more the exception than the rule.

For the media and later for the public, the build-up prior to the Iraq war and later the war itself was a time of learning that:

- Censorship in time of war is readily accepted by the public, if only grudgingly by the media;
- Debate over public policy whether in Congress, on the street, or on campuses is necessarily complex and requires considerable context;
- War coverage is necessarily multifaceted and complex, requiring stories about politics, economics, geography, and social custom;
- New technology associated with the gathering and transmission of news by satellite is both a blessing and a curse. It brings information faster and provides better visual display, but it does not necessarily build public support in or for the media's overall performance; and
- Relative newcomers to the news business such as CNN could outdistance better-heeled broadcast and print competitors through a competitive edge aided by technology and assured by economics.

These and other lessons of war would condition the media as the war emerged not just as so much jingoistic talk but as a harsh and inevitable reality.

Ironically, for some media executives early public opinion soundings seemed contradictory. As one editor asked plaintively, "How can 85% of the people support the war; 80% support the president and only 60% approve of us?" The old refrain of "Why do they hate us out there?," which led to the media credibility crisis of 1984, was raised anew.

Whether the role of the media in informing the public about the Gulf War and in setting an agenda for understanding it will be found to have had a greater impact and influence than in the past, is something researchers will have to tell us later. But this may be the first important test in our new "age of information," when cities are wired and public communication is more abundant than ever before.

35. No, TV Has Not Killed the Print Medium[†]

Hours after the Persian Gulf War opened in prime time on television for most Americans, a journalism professor at the University of Maryland told his colleagues that they had just witnessed "the death of print."

Suddenly newspapers and news magazines seemed irrelevant, helpless in the face of minute-by-minute changes in the opening hours of the war to cover it in any satisfactory way. Newspaper reporters and their editors went to bed on January 15 knowing that what they had prepared for their readers that day would be out-of-date by morning. This had happened before, of course, but never so dramatically.

In a world where technology determines the rapid delivery of news and information, newspapers appeared unable to cope with people's need for immediate intelligence about the was. Newsmagazines seemingly faced an even more difficult task. After all, news is a perishable commodity and has no more value than spoiled fruit if it comes late.

Research conducted the day after the war began seemed to back up the "death of print" prediction. Not that newspapers and magazines would fold their tents and secede from the communication industry, but the numbers raised serious questions. One study, conducted by Birch/Scarborough, asked 2,000 people in 105 markets how they kept up with the war news. The results for print seemed

† This chapter originally appeared as an article in *Newsday*, February 7, 1991.

devastating, as 55% said television, 23% named radio, and only 9% mentioned newspapers.

Newspapers and magazines, however, have been discounted before. Nearly 30 years ago, the Canadian media guru Marshall McLuhan observed that the visual electronic media were infinitely more compelling and involving than books, newspapers, and magazines. He also predicted "the death of print." This idea was reinforced at the time of the assassination of President John F. Kennedy. A stunned nation sat in front of television sets watching what was then called live coverage for four days. Commercial announcements were suspended and television won hands down as the most important source of news about that national tragedy. At that time television scored another victory as well. It became more than a medium of information. It became a companion, a dependable member of the family, that provided a cathartic focal point for individual and collective grief.

Still, newspapers and magazines did not die out as a medium. Instead, then and now they did what television as yet cannot do: serve as a true sense-maker, an integrator of information, an interpreter and analyst. Newspaper stories about the Gulf War were carefully labeled, so that readers could see how they fit together, like spokes within a wheel. They integrated current and background information.

Although television and its broadband companion cable are transmitting news more rapidly and efficiently, the print media are using electronic means to gather and edit news more effectively. For the public this means more and better information, even though it comes later than TV.

Newspapers have also benefited from advances in computer graphics, and for the public this means better maps and schematic diagrams of the war, visual material that does not appear ephemerally on a screen but can be assiduously studied in greater detail than television can provide.

Television's great strength to date in the war—that of immediacy and compelling real time reports—is also a weakness. The public, though being taken inside a moving story, sees the journalistic process at work. This means that fragmented reports and images, some of them accurate and on target, others wrong and discarded minutes later, give the viewer the same raw material that journalists use in assembling their report. For instance, several of the early reports of Scud missile attacks were at first partly confirmed, only to be revealed later as false. CNN is the best example of this, taking a real-time, "you are there" approach to the news that, though gripping and compelling during action, can be dull, misleading, and unsatisfying at other times. The

more conventional "big three" networks, after initially trying continuous broadcasting, reverted to expanded hour-long national new's
programs. These usually succeed in more thoughtfully integrating
material. On the other hand, they still have little time for substantive
analysis or opinion, still mostly taboo in broadcasting.

Opinion is a print media specialty. There are editorial pages, letters to
the editor, op-ed pages,and commentaries. And although readers may
not agree with a particular viewpoint, it gives them a pertinent point of
departure for their own views. One can count on most newspapers to
comment, criticize and analyze the war and other events. Only radio
competes at all with print as a medium of opinion, mainly through talk
shows. While radio is a safety valve for some people's opinions, it is too
sporadic and fragmented to be much of a sense-maker—with rare exceptions, such as National Public Radio.

Not to be forgotten is that although television gives a sense that
the war is so important that other news is mostly crowded out,
newspapers and magazines, while covering war, do a better job of
keeping track of nonwar news.

It would be a mistake to discount the newspaper or the newsmag-
azine just yet. They live in a different, more varied media world in
which competing electronic voices—more than ever before—vie for
public attention. Each medium has its special place, its unique
characteristics and capabilities. The Persian Gulf War may speed
their redefinition, but the viewing public will benefit no matter what
happens. In the end, readers, listeners, and viewers will make their
choices, but if experience is a teacher, newspapers covering war (and
everything else) will be with us for a long time.

36. Defining Times for the Mass Media[†]

President Bush used the word *defining* carefully in describing the
possible consequences of the Persian Gulf War. Because the stakes
for all participants in the war were so great, it was easy to see why

---

† *Communiqué* column, February 1991 (monthly newsletter of FFMSC).

such consequences define the futures of nations, alliances, and individual leaders. For the communications media, the war with Iraq came at a time when the distinguishing characteristics of each modern mass communication tool were seen in stark relief. In large part because the war "opened" on prime-time television, the power and immediacy of that medium has been praised and scrutinized. Never before could people watch a war in what is now called "real time." There are no more delays to transport or process film or tape, but a here-and-now window on war from the scene of action or close to it.

Ironically, in the first days of the war, television was not particularly a picture medium; instead, it was a medium for transmitting information from briefings, reporters' observations, and experts' opinions. What pictures there were came mainly from pool footage, approved by each country's military and government censors. From a media perspective, these initial days of the war were a triumph for our newest mass medium—cable. Cable News Network (CNN), a relative newcomer to the family of news "networks," attracted the most attention, winning praise and criticism for its performance. In the process of its war coverage, CNN also treated the idea of convergence of technologies by not only serving homes, offices, and institutions wired for cable but also by providing a service to independent broadcast stations, and even to affiliates of the established big three networks. The upstart cable network also claimed another distinction that was once held only by great national newspapers and wire services: Their broadcasts were seen as "the American viewpoint" in government ministries the world over, and in international hotels where global commerce transactions are made.

During this conflict, television again confirmed what has been true for a long time—that it is the preeminent source of information for most Americans. Though newspapers may have lost that role with the advent of television, it is evident with their war coverage that they still play an important part as the great quasi-permanent sense-makers by providing coherent, integrated news reports, maps and charts, and analysis and interpretation in a way not yet possible for television. Though few people now rely on newspapers and newsmagazines as a primary source for immediate news, for anyone who truly wants to be informed these media are vital.

Radio also showed its mettle during the Gulf conflict, not only with regular news reports but also with its important interactive function, most often in the form of talk shows that let listeners talk back to the host, the government, and the media. Through much of the crisis, war coverage by all major media was constrained by severe censorship, ostensibly erected to prevent the free flow of information to the enemy about military operations. Due to censorship, however, we really never became aware of all that was happening in the Persian Gulf. Yet within those limits on information, all of our major media devoted enormous resources to provide what is mostly a public interest function—that of informing the public. In some instances they did this with little hope of a return on the investment, thereby demonstrating that our media still have that curious mixture that makes them part commercial enterprise and part public servant.

37. CNN: A Network Comes of Age[†]

When the history of the Persian Gulf War is written, there is little doubt that one of the key players will be Cable News Network. From the beginning of the conflict on January 16, CNN was not only an important observer and reporter of the events of the war but the object of much discussion as well.

Not only was CNN taken seriously but it also out-distanced the major broadcast networks both with the instantaneous nature of its coverage and in the resourcefulness of its people. What was once a minor-league video ticker-tape was at last maturing as a news organization and as a competitor to the Big Three networks.

This was a far cry from the days when the Big Three networks sneered at CNN as second-rate news on the cheap. And it seemed to end the once-prevalent ridicule that this relatively new entry in the field of electronically delivered news had only recently suffered.

Only three years ago, in the midst of severe network news budget cuts and downsizing, then-CBS News president Howard Stringer playfully asked the audience at a Gannett Center conference at

---

† This chapter originally appeared March 1991 in *Multichannel News*.

Columbia University, "If CNN is the answer, what is the question?" Members of the audience chuckled at Stringer's clever jibe.

The question in the case of the Gulf War, it seems, is: Who can deliver the news most expeditiously and efficiently to the American audience? And the answer in many instances was CNN.

Importantly, CNN, once only a cable service with no real over-the-air broadcast presence, had slowly become the "network feed" for many independent, nonaffiliated stations. At the outset of the Persian Gulf War, CNN also benefitted from defecting Big Three affiliates, who abandoned their own network offerings to give their viewers the real time coverage of CNN. And though this involved only a few stations, most of whom quickly returned to their own network's offerings, the fact that they turned to CNN at all was a profoundly important statement and a recognition of CNN's pre-eminence as a newsgathering organization with something dramatically different to offer the viewer.

The night of January 16, 1991, may be remembered as the night that CNN demonstrated the concept of convergence, wherein the lines between cable and broadcasting as well as print were blurred. After all, CNN not only was reported about on television and radio but also became the source of newspaper and magazine reports as well.

And who could have asked for better advertising than CNN got in comments on other networks both by anchors and commentators, not to mention the secretary of defense and chairman of the Joint Chiefs of Staff. All seemed to be paraphrasing what Will Rogers used to say about newspapers: "All I know is what I have seen on CNN."

Not only was CNN a major source for government officials, diplomats, and military commanders but we also learned that it was being watched by the other side, by none other than Saddam Hussein himself.

So not only was CNN commanding a larger and larger national audience in the United States, where it would eventually come close to beating (in the ratings) CBS News, which trailed ABC and NBC news operations, but it also was the "wire service" for an elite audience in international hotels and among government leaders in other countries.

CNN achieved a distinction no other electronic medium in the United States had ever enjoyed—that of being seen as "the American view" by an overseas audience. Many U.S. media analysts and journalists either have forgotten or simply do not know that the U.S. networks have little presence overseas. That is, they simply do not reach appreciable audiences in other countries. They may offer global coverage, but it is clearly for American viewers, as there is no global audience for their fare—at least not yet.

CNN, on the other hand, was achieving what the *New York Times* and the Associated Press had previously enjoyed—access to an elite audience in other countries who looked at the service as an instant electronic wire service.

And, of course, they saw it as an American news organization mostly addressing its reports to an American audience. Still, they could tune-in with the American audience and have easy access to reports on the war. No doubt this influenced the Iraqi leader and his ministers when they granted CNN exclusive rights to transmit from Baghdad while other networks and news organizations were denied access.

The Gulf War has given the television viewing audience a much more conscious image and understanding of CNN, which has demonstrated its professionalism in delivering the news and its resourcefulness in breaking stories first and making arrangements to keep its reporters and field producers in places off-limits to other newsgathering organizations.

Although there would later be many complaints about CNN's cavalier use of the work of other networks' reporters (as in the pool coverage) and whether its reports from Baghdad were, in fact, "aiding and abetting the enemy," no one could deny that CNN had given traditional broadcasters fits and had even for a time beaten them at their own game. Tom Brokaw's unprecedented interview with Bernard Shaw, for example, was proof positive that CNN was not only covering the news but also on the agenda itself.

Naturally, with a growing audience, CNN was quick to raise its advertising rates, sometimes as much as 500% for primetime commercials. And although CNN's enviable triumph should not be undervalued, it is also fair to say that the network's vigorous coverage raised disturbing questions. Was there, for example, too much "coverage" and too little "reporting?" That is, did CNN do too much raw feed in real time without rigor in fact-checking and analysis? Did CNN contribute to the illusions of news-unedited, rather than convey a high-caliber but often subtly edited report more common in the other networks? Did CNN opt for immediacy over quality control? Was Peter Arnett's coverage of the Iraqi point-of-view "propaganda from the enemy camp" as some have charged?

These are questions that are being hotly debated, but they do not diminish CNN's emergence as a major newsgathering force, one that is efficient and cost-effective, in part because of its newness, lack of unions, and corporate and operational locations in Atlanta, where costs are lower than in New York. There is little doubt that the recent CNN triumph has both angered and frightened the Big Three networks, as their reactions have demonstrated.

Whether the Persian Gulf War will give a much larger viewing public the CNN habit, whether viewers and other news organizations will become dependent on CNN the way they are either indirectly or directly dependent on the AP is not yet known. That will inevitably be tied to economics and, specifically, profits. The other networks began their lives as loss leaders for broadcasting services that brought entertainment and sports. CNN, on the other hand, follows the model of a newspaper, a commercial enterprise, that markets a tangible commodity called news.

Whatever happens, the cable industry and the broadcast industry, as well as the public, will be watching with great interest and even some concern.

38. Media's Commitment to News: Will It Survive?[†]

Almost every media industry trade journal in the late 1980s carried news of layoffs in America's newsrooms. News organizations, with their reliance on advertising, subscriptions, and user fees, were not immune to the 1991 recession that burdened the economy. Profits were down and cost-cutting measures of all kinds were imposed. With the first major personnel cutbacks in newsrooms since the 1970s, questions arose about what the public would lose in the process. In 1991, extraordinary coverage of the Persian Gulf War sorely tested and taxed newsroom budgets. Still, in spite of overall

---

† *Communiqué* column, April 1991 (monthly newsletter of FFMSC).

economic gloom, America's publishers and broadcasters overspent their budgets as they allocated resources to Gulf coverage. Though there is still much to examine and evaluate in what these resources yielded, there can be no question that the news media were committed to this great and compelling story.

What happened in Gulf coverage also reinforced claims of media owners that they really do care about news and that the rush of market values into newsrooms had not cut off their fundamental concern about covering it. In fact, some critics who have decried network news and other media reductions in newsroom personnel and budgets were pleasantly surprised by the news expenditures. Even though additional advertising did not necessarily follow on the heels of augmented news coverage, television viewership and newspaper and magazine readership were up considerably. This seems to reinforce the idea that vigorous commitment to hard news that people care about will command expanded audiences. Over the long term a commitment to news will also attract advertising and could allow newspapers and magazines to increase their subscription and newsstand prices. When people really care about the news, they will not only pay attention to television but also rush out to buy more newspapers and magazines. That this happened in spite of the recession speaks well for the values of our media and the fundamental commitment in a crunch to serving the public interest, which is exactly what expanded war coverage did.

Whether the media's owners and their managers can find a formula to translate the war coverage success into peacetime and domestic affairs remains to be seen. The newsroom cutbacks and other economic measures since the war do not seem to have the same ringing commitment to news and information. The euphoria about the chance to cover a war was felt in every newsroom. During the war, the tempo of news operations quickened and there was excitement in the air. Now it remains to be tested whether and how the basic truth about people's desire for pertinent, salient information that affects their lives and the lives of others around the world can be turned into a renewed commitment to news that people can experience, appreciate and apply. It is to that task that resourceful and responsible newspeople ought to be dedicated, remembering that often the best ideas for new publications and other "media products" have emerged in just such periods.

References

Abramson, J. B., Arterton, F. C., & Orren, G. R. (1988). *The electronic commonwealth & the impact of new media technologies on democratic policies.* New York: Basic Books.

Auletta, K. (1991). *Three blind mice: How the networks lost their way.* New York: Random House.

Avery, R. K., & Eason, D. (1991). *Critical perspectives on media and society.* New York: Guilford.

Bagdikian, B. H. (1990). *The media monopoly* (3rd ed.). Boston: Beacon Press.

Beville, H. M., Jr. (1988). *Audience ratings: Radio, television, cable* (Rev. ed.). Hillsdale, NJ: Lawrence Erlbaum.

Bollinger, L. C. (1991). *Images of a free press.* Chicago, IL: University of Chicago Press.

Bradley, S., & Hausman, J. (Eds.). (1989). *Future competition telecommunications.* Boston, MA: Harvard Business School Press.

Brand, S. (1987). *The media lab: Inventing the future at MIT.* New York: Viking.

Brody, E. W. *Communication tomorrow: New audiences, new technologies, new media.* New York: Praeger.

Clurman, R. M. (1987). *Beyond malice: The media's years of reckoning.* New Brunswick: Transaction.

Cose, E. (1989). *The press.* New York: William Morrow.

Dennis, E., & Rivers, W. L. (1971). *Other voices: The new journalism in America.* New York: Canfield.

Diamond, E. *The media show: The changing face of the news, 1985-1990.* Cambridge, MA: MIT Press.

Entman, R. (1989). *Democracy without citizens: Media and the decay of American politics.* New York: Oxford University Press.

Foote, J. S. (1990). *Television access and political power: The networks, the presidency, and the loyal opposition.* New York: Praeger.

Ganley, O. H. (1989). *To inform or to control? The new communications networks* (2nd ed.). Norwood, NJ: Ablex.

Gleason, T. W. (1989). *The watchdog concept: The press and the courts in nineteenth-century America.* Ames, IA: Iowa State University Press.

Goldberg, R., & Goldberg, G. J. (1990). *The anchors: Rather, Jennings, Brokaw, and the TV news business.* New York: Birch Lane.

Hanson, J., & Narula, U. (1990). *New communication technologies in developing countries.* Hillsdale, NJ: Lawrence Erlbaum.

Iyengar, S., & Kinder, D. R. (1987). *News that matters: Television and American opinion.* Chicago: University of Chicago Press.

Kubey, R., & Csekszentmihalyi, M. (1990). *Television and the quality of life: How viewing shapes everyday experience.* Hillsale, NJ: Lawrence Erlbaum.

Lavrakas, P. J., & Holley, J. K. (1991). *Polling and presidential election coverage.* Newbury Park, CA: Sage.

Linsky, M. (1986). *Impact: How the press affects federal policymaking.* New York: Norton.

MacDonald, J. F. *One nation under television: The rise and decline of network TV.* New York: Pantheon.

Manoff, R. K., & Schudson, M. (Eds.). (1986). *Reading the news.* New York: Pantheon.

Meyrowitz, J. (1985). *No sense of place: The impact of electronic media on social behavior.* New York: Oxford University Press.

Pool, I. D. S. (1990). *Technology without boundaries.* Cambridge, MA: Harvard University Press.

Postman, N. (1985). *Amusing ourselves to death: Public discourse in the age of show business.* New York: Viking Penguin.

Postman, N. (1988). *Conscientious objections.* New York: Knopf.

Saxby, S. (1990). *The age of information.* New York: New York University Press.

Sloan, W. D. (1990). *The media in America: A history.* Worthington, OH: Publishing Horizons.

Wanniski, J. (Ed.). (1991). *1991 media guide: A critical review of the media.* Morristown, NJ: Polyconomics/Repap.

Weaver, D. H., & Wilhoit, G. C. (1991). *The American journalist: A portrait of U.S. news people and their work* (2nd ed.). Bloomington, IN: Indiana University Press.

Weiss, C., & Singer, E. (1988). *Reporting of social science in the national media.* New York: Russell Sage.

Index

French Revolution, 68
Friendly, Fred W., 18

Garfield, James A., 80
Gartner, Michael, 137
General Electric, 11
Geraldo, 17, 26, 46
Gerbner, George, 52
Ghiglione, Loren, 155
Gilliam, Dorothy, 136
Glasnost, 46, 54, 55, 56, 57, 58, 106
Globe, The, 136
Gorbachev, Mikhail, 16, 46, 47, 49, 50, 54, 58
Gosteleradio, 55
Great Depression, 131
Greek and Roman Generals, 103
Greeley, Horace, 9
Greenfield, Jeff, 126

Hachette S. A., 116, 123
Halberstam, David, 169
Halliburton, Richard, 42
Hallin, Daniel, 52
Hart, Gary, 136
Harvard University, 137
Hearst, William Randolph, 162
Hirsch, E. D., 86
Hopkins, Mark, 80
"Horrors of the Madhouse," 139
House of Representatives, U.S., 167
Hudson, Rock, 31
Hull House, 148
Hurricane Hugo, 28
Hussein, Saddam, 145, 167, 175

IBM, 159
Industrial Revolution, 15
Information Age, 15, 16, 20, 23
"Interceptor," 158
International Communication Association, 77
International Institute of Communications, 58
International Press Institute, 58
Iron Curtain, 8

Internal Revenue Service, 14
Izvestia, 55, 56

Jackson, The Reverend Jesse, 134
Jennings, Peter, 29
"Jimmy's World," 104
Johnson, Lyndon B., 81, 138
Joint Chiefs of Staff, 175
Justice Department, U.S., 14

Kennedy, John F., 137, 138, 171
Kennedy Compound, 136, 137, 138
Kerner Commission, 133, 135
KGB, 47, 51
Khomeini, Ayatollah Ruhollah, 111, 112
Khrushchev, Nikita, 49
King Tutankhamen's Tomb, 48
Kinsella, James, 31
Knightley, Phillip, 145, 168
Know-Nothingism, 108

"L.A. Law," 22
Laptev, Ivan, 56
Lasswell, Harold, 19, 147
Lazy Susan, 97
Le Page's Glue, 160
Lenin, Vladimir Ilyich, 49
Library of Congress, U.S., 155
Life, 139
Lippmann, Walter, 19, 131
Log, The, 80
Los Angeles Times, 18
Luce, Henry, 27, 36, 125
Luddite, 121

Ma Bell, 19
MacNeil/Lehrer NewsHour, 161
Malcolm, Janet, 162
Mandela, Nelson, 26, 31
Mapplethorpe, Robert, 147
"March of Time," 36, 125
Marcos, Ferdinand, 28
Markle Foundation, 109
McCarthyism, 77

About the Author

Everette E. Dennis is Executive Director of the Freedom Forum Media Studies Center at Columbia University, and Vice-President of the Freedom Forum (formerly the Gannett Foundation). Formerly he was Dean of the School of Journalism at the University of Oregon and Professor of Journalism and Director of Graduate Studies at the University of Minnesota. A Past President of the Association for Education in Journalism and Mass Communication and Director of the Project on the Future of Journalism Education, he is author, coauthor, or editor of 22 books and numerous articles, including *Reshaping the Media*, *The Cost of Libel*, *Media and the Environment*, *Beyond the Cold War*, *The Media Society*, and *Understanding Mass Communication*. He has also held fellowships at Harvard Law School, the Nieman Foundation, and the John F. Kennedy School of Government at Harvard University. He is a trustee of the International Museum of Photography at Eastman House, a counsellor of the American Antiquarian Society, and a member of the Council on Foreign Relations.